AAARGH TO ZIZZ

135 DRAMA GAMES

by

Graeme K. Talboys

Dramatic Lines*

Aaargh to Zizz
text copyright © Graeme K. Talboys

This book is intended to provide resource material
for teachers and students in schools and colleges.
No permission is required for amateur use.
Applications for professional use should be made to:

Dramatic Lines
PO Box 201
Twickenham
TW2 5RQ
England

A CIP record for this book is
available from the British Library

ISBN 0 9537770 5 7

Aaargh to Zizz
first edition published in 2002
second edition published in 2007
by
Dramatic Lines
Twickenham England

Printed by the Dramatic Lines Press
Twickenham England

Contents

for Barbara

Acknowledgements

These games are intended primarily for use with children, although many can be used with adults as well. They have proven to be remarkably flexible over the years and this made them invaluable in the help they gave to the children I worked with.

Many of these games were learnt in the playing. I would, therefore, like to thank the Drama Department staff who taught me at St Peter's College, Saltley (1972-1975) along with my year group, as well as all those children and staff at Madeley Court, Shropshire (1975-1979) who first brought them to my attention. In particular, I would like to thank Howard Mullen under whose tutelage I had the opportunity to develop this interest and David Griffiths who has encouraged my work through the years.

It is certain that this collection would never have seen the light of day without the encouragement and selflessness of my wife. To her I offer my especial thanks.

Clas Myrddin
January 2002

Introduction

Games, such as those featured in this book, are a structured form of play. The importance of play is more widely recognised than ever before and offers an increasingly fascinating area of study for the psychologist of child and adult alike. All children play at some time or other, if only in their heads. Many continue to play into their teens and early adulthood, evolving the games they play to more sophisticated levels whilst turning gradually to the sort of games they will play as adults.

Yet play is something which still defies definition. We usually know it when we see it. We invariably recognise it as such when we do it. But if we stand back and attempt to define it, we rapidly experience difficulties. There are so many variables involved that once they are taken out of the picture we seem to be left with nothing at all.

One of the major problems is that play is sensitive to time and place. That is, an activity that at one time and place may be regarded as play can, although identical in form, be regarded as something else in different circumstances. A person who is running may be playing. But running can be a matter of survival. The activity is the same. Therefore it is not in the activity that a definition of play can reside.

If not in the activity itself, then it may well be in the motivation for an activity that the key to a definition lies. Perhaps one of the oldest and most popular views about the motivation for play is that it is the discharge of an excess of energy - of which children always seem to have a great deal. This excess arises, so the theory goes, because children are free of the concerns of adult life, and protected from them by adults. Such an idea came from the early psychological studies of children made in extremely limited and comfortable circumstances.

After all, you can see children in refugee camps playing games, even after a long day fighting for scraps of food.

Instinct is also considered a motivation and lies close to the idea that play is an apprenticeship for adult life. This derives mostly from a study of animals other than humans. There is more than an element of truth in this. Just as young animals mimic their elders, children mimic their parents and other adults and practise skills that will make them successful independent adults. But it is a long way from the whole story - even in non-human animals.

From the apprenticeship model grew certain theories of play as a form of condensed social evolution. Much as the foetus in the womb goes through residual stages that resemble the evolution of life, children, it was thought, go through an accelerated social evolution from 'barbarism' to 'civilisation'. This too was prevalent in those days when a great degree of cultural and social superiority was assumed by those making the theories.

All these theories, and many more besides, represent a large investment of time on the part of investigators. Yet, as with all fields of study into activity and the human mind, nothing conclusive has been formulated. There are no wholly satisfactory theories as to how play came about in the first place and, given that it does exist precisely what it is. Each of the theories stands, more or less, on its own criteria but none of them offer a complete picture.

Be all that as it may, what we can say with certainty is that play is a major and beneficial part of a child's life. It certainly refreshes both mentally and physically. Sleep and rest are both necessary but play, as an interesting and active participation in life is more refreshing than idleness. This has as much to do with social cohesion and a sense of belonging as it does with exercise of the mind and body. That is why play needs to be physically active as well as mentally stimulating and socially interactive.

Play also acts as a safety-valve for emotion. Children, particularly adolescents, have extremely rich emotional lives. Sometimes the fare is a bit too rich, especially where emotions are being experienced for the first time. In play, emotional turmoil can be given a chance to resolve into more balanced and less confusing fare; new emotions can be explored or put aside for later; they can even be expressed in controlled situations where such activity is tolerated (subject to safeguards outlined in the Notes).

Not knowing wholly what play is, per se, nor what motivates it on a day to day basis, does not mean we do not understand its long term purpose. It is not merely for refreshment, emotional redaction, and relaxation even though they may be its immediate principal driving forces. More importantly, and in the long term, play is a major means by which children experiment with and explore the world about them in a safe and structured way.

Play allows them - in relatively safe situations from which they can withdraw at will - to build, alter, discard and rebuild internal models and maps of the world by which they can navigate through the increasing complexities of life. This is a process that never ends. The more detailed the map or model, the easier it becomes to explore further and add increasingly sophisticated levels of detail. Furthermore, as the person who is exploring grows and matures that person requires different things of the map or model and sees it from different perspectives - which requires yet more exploration.

It is not necessary to know why play exists or what its exact role is, however, to recognise that it is of vital importance to children for their physical, emotional, social, and intellectual development and well being.

Through play children develop confidence and experience to fit them for their adult life to come. Through play, they mature and evolve.

There is a second side to this coin. For, as play may be considered the engine that drives maturity and evolution, forms of play also evolve and mature. If the desire to play at a childish level is suppressed and not exhausted, then the kind of play indulged in does not evolve. What is good in children becomes a distorted, inappropriate and sometimes dangerous element in adolescent and adult life.

By observing natural play it is possible, without the need for deep analysis and psychological insight, to see how to construct play to help fulfil what is lacking in the life of a child. The games in this book are a part of that process, where natural forms of play are structured to focus on the development of particular skills.

In many cases it is children who have done this for themselves. Many of the games in this book could be classed as traditional. They have evolved from loose or free play into structured formats, providing pleasant fare to feed certain hungers.

Some people feel that games, having a rigid structure, place too many constraints on development. Others feel that the structure is an adult imposition on children. Such advocates of free development are, I believe, misguided in that they do not understand the nature of freedom. Freedom is relative rather than absolute. The co-operative nature of games (groups must co-operate in the venture even if the game is competitive) is one of the things that helps establish this principle in the mind of the child. Besides, adults have a responsibility to guide children into adulthood - which is not the same as imposing adult values upon them.

Games, by their very nature, are not set in stone. One of the things that must be borne in mind is that a game is something that has variety. It may need to keep a basic structure in order to maintain its integrity or identity, but beyond that, each game can be used and adapted so that individual needs can be catered for. Extra rules can be added to increase complexity and structure and thus diversify or tighten up skills, or focus those already developed into the development of new ones.

Children, too, have an instinct for this. Altering games to make them more fun often results in them focusing on skills they need to develop. There are, of course, cases where the structure of a game will be counter-productive to what you aim for. In that case it is not the game that is at fault. It is up to you, as the controlling influence, to be aware of the levels of development within the group or groups that you work with and plan accordingly. There are times when games will be the most appropriate route forward. There will be other times when they will not.

It must be recognised, however, that children need security. The basic rules and the physical set up of the game are constants which players know and can feel happy about. They can be comfortable within the limited world that is the game because they, and all other players, know what the limits are. Within this circumscription they gain, to a certain extent, control of their own fate.

With this basic security established it becomes easier for individuals to improvise and explore as well as take risks - becoming involved in activities the child might otherwise avoid. Inherent in this are the learning processes that exist: the development of skills required to play the game and to improve that play along with more general skills of judgement, memory, response, reaction, observation, listening, perception, concentration, numeracy and literacy, co-ordination, trust, and so on.

All the aforementioned skills will be carried away from the game situation at increasingly developed levels and applied to other aspects of the child's life and education. And they will transfer because they are learnt subliminally. It is not the main aim of any game to impart these skills, they simply evolve because the playing of the game is fun and to participate more fully the child exercises and develops these skills. This is unlike specific and subject orientated aspects of knowledge which children sometimes have difficulty in transferring from one subject area to another.

A particular case in point is the beneficial effect of traditional games on playground behaviour. Bullying is a problem that is much to the fore at present. Many primary schools are finding that a revival of traditional playground games (as opposed to the mimicking of computer games and the acquisition of sets of cards) provide an atmosphere in which aggressive behaviour and bullying are easier to prevent.

For all that, the most important thing to remember is that a game is just that - a game. They can be used as part of a developmental programme but for children they are fun and that is how they should be approached otherwise they will fail. In other words, understand the many levels of learning that can take place within their playing, but never try to use them as a cover for this. Hidden agendas are extremely difficult to keep hidden from children, especially when you start to tamper with aspects of their world. Understand what they are and make room for them, knowing they are valid within an educational environment.

You may recognise some of the games that follow and I make no claims for originality. Although many of the games can be used with adults, they are intended primarily for use with children. I used them as a Drama teacher mostly in formal Drama sessions, but they will work equally well during informal sessions such as clubs or parties. In the years that I used them, they proved to be remarkably flexible - from warm up to cool down, inspiration to conclusion, deadly serious to purest fun. These games were invaluable in the help they gave to the children I worked with.

The games grew closer to the core of my work as I saw their value, yet because of their very nature, I never allowed them to become the be-all and end-all of that work. I do, however, know that the games all work with a large variety of children from nine to eighteen years of age covering a large part of the social and educational spectrum.

It is up to you how you use these games but above all else, enjoy them.

Notes

Before playing any of these games it would be as well to take cognizance of a number of general principles, especially if you are new to working with groups in this way.

- These games need to be played in a fairly large room that is free of obstacles other than those required for the game. A Drama Studio, School Hall or Village Hall are ideal. If the room has blackout curtains and variable light control, so much the better although these are not essential. Some of the games can also be played outside where a clearly defined playing area, such as a tennis court, can be provided.

- Games are cooperative ventures, despite the competitive element that some of them contain. They should be approached in this light otherwise they become a seeding ground for the expenditure of a great deal of hostility, negating any worth they may otherwise have had.

- I always worked to a very strict rule that no matter what work was being done it should NEVER be used by members of the group as an excuse or a cover for things that might be going on between them on the 'outside'. The Drama studio was 'neutral' territory. As some of the games are extremely physical you should consider playing them only with groups you know and can trust to play without using the game as a cover for aggressive behaviour.

- Some of the games, such as *OVER THE WALL* might be deemed dangerous. All those chairs could collapse. Children hurtling around trying to change places could bump into one another. You have to be certain about what you are doing and of the capabilities of the group before you attempt such things. Keep a sharp eye open for the usual suspects and pull them out straight away if they get over excited.

- Many of these games rely on what you might call 'fair play'. If someone says they saw someone doing something they must have done so, and the person seen must accept this. In *ELIMINATION* for example, the volunteer cannot change the object that was first thought of as the game goes on.

- In games where players are eliminated for making a mistake, a useful variation is to give everyone three lives and thus, three chances at being out. This is especially useful for groups with members who have a hard time accepting failure, even in games.

- If a game requires forfeits, or you prefer them to someone being out of the game altogether, there are a number of variations. Simply missing one or more turns is the easiest and perhaps the best to be used in situations where confidence is an issue. Other forms of forfeit such as the peas in *YES AND NO* also work well.

- Many or all of these games can be adapted to other ends than that of pure fun. For example, the game *CONCENTRATION* can be used in teaching situations to calm a group at the beginning and/or end of a teaching session.

- I have also given a number of variations with some of the games. As you play, you and the groups you work with will, no doubt, think of many more.

With the obvious exception of *TWO BY TWO,* which is best suited to younger children, these games can be played at varying levels of sophistication with nine year olds and upwards. How and when, why and at what age you introduce them to a group is entirely dependent on you and on the group. There are no hard and fast rules, but it is important that the element of fun remains paramount.

Equipment

If you want to play all the games in this collection you will need to make you have all of the following equipment to hand. Most of it is fairly straightforward and the more specialised pieces can be used in other contexts or for other games. Cards, cuttings and lists will last much longer if they can be mounted on card and laminated.

The game number is suffixed 'V' if equipment is only required to play a variation of the main game.

GAMES THAT DO NOT REQUIRE EQUIPMENT

16. 17. 29. 30. 35. 41. 44. 47. 48. 70. 88. 91. 92. 96. 99. 100. 104. 105. 112. 118. 119.

EQUIPMENT REQUIRED FOR GAMES

- **Chairs** - Minimum requirement is 1 chair per game and the maximum requirement for any game is one chair for each group member but Games 36. 68. require 1 chair for each group member plus 1 extra chair.
- 1. 2. 3. 4. 5. 6. 7. 8. 9. 10. 11. 12. 13. 14. 15. 18. 19. 20. 21. 22. 23. 24. 25. 26. 28. 31. 32. 33. 36. 37. 38. 39. 40. 41v. 42. 43. 45. 49. 50. 51. 52. 53. 54. 55. 56. 57. 58. 59. 60. 61. 62. 63. 64. 65. 66. 67. 68. 69. 72. 73. 74. 75. 76. 77. 78. 79. 80. 81. 82. 83. 84. 85. 86. 87. 89. 90. 93. 94. 95. 98. 101. 102. 103. 106. 107. 108. 109. 110. 111. 113. 115. 116. 117. 120. 121. 123. 124. 125. 127. 128. 129. 130. 131. 132. 133. 134.

- **Alphabet Cards** - a pack of 26 cards each card clearly printed with a single letter of the alphabet. It would be useful to have several of these so that packs can be combined to make a set of consonants and a set of vowels.
  2. 51v. 53. 64. 65v. 86.

- **A box of pencils** - enough for one for each player.
  4. 5. 19. 25. 26.

- **Paper** - given the nature of its use it would be best to collect scrap and cut it to a handy size.
  4. 5. 19. 25. 26.

- **Two small sturdy boxes** - into which pieces of paper can be put and subsequently drawn out.
  4. 5. 19. 126.

- **Occupation Cards** - a set of cards each with the name of an occupation like nurse, miner, and so on. The more of these the better.
  9. 78v.

- **Tennis balls** - at least two of these in different colours.
  10. 14v. 62. 74.

- **Chalk.**
  13*. 73.
  *or masking tape.

- **A small block of smooth wood** - about 30mm square and 150mm long to represent a piece of cheese.
  14.

- **A collection of small objects** -that will produce distinctive sounds.
  24v.

- **Couples cards** - a set of cards in which well known couples are represented one name on each card. For example, one card has Laurel and another Hardy; one card has Solomon and another Sheba; one has R2D2 and another C3P0, and so on. Each card should have the hooky part of a piece of Velcro stuck to its back so that the cards can be attached to clothing. There are other forms of couples other than people that can be made up into sets of cards: -

  a) instead of naming well known people use pictures of them.
  b) pairs of objects like lock and key, bow and arrow, horse and cart, button and buttonhole.
  c) pairs of geometric shapes.
  d) similes split in half like as bold - as brass, as busy as - a bee.
  e) words and their definitions.
  f) capital cities and their countries.
  g) book titles and authors.
  ..... and so on.
  27.

- **A bunch of old keys.**
  28.

- **A room with a blackout and variable light control.**
  34*. 83. 97.
  *Blackout is useful but not essential as Game 34 can be played without.

- **A table.**
  36. 81. 83*. 103. 129.
  *Game 83 can make use of a number of tables if these are available.

- **A Feely Box** - this can be made quite easily from a large sturdy cardboard box from your local supermarket. Remove the top and cut a hole in the bottom big enough to put a hand, wrist and forearm through but small enough to prevent whoever does so from seeing what might be placed in the box. Put the box on a table with the open top facing the group so everyone can see in.

36.

- **Everyday objects** - You will need a collection of everyday objects to place in the Feely Box. These should be changed frequently and kept hidden in another box so no one can see what they are.

  36.

- **Number pack 1 - 100** - a set of one hundred cards each printed clearly with a single number from one to one hundred.

  39.

- **Group cards** - a set of cards in which groups of names are represented one name on each card. For example, in a set of three - one card has Superman, one Wonderwoman, and one Spiderman; in a set of four - one card has Clubs, one has Spades, one has Hearts, and one has Diamonds, and so on. Each card should have the hooky part of a piece of Velcro stuck to its back so that the cards can be attached to clothing.

  46.

- **Knick-knacks** - pairs of small everyday objects of similar shape and size but of different appearance.

  62v.

- **A collection of small objects** - that you can distribute amongst your pockets. These do not have to be unusual but should include things other than the ones you normally carry about with you.

  67. 81.

- **A Magnificent Dido** - your guess is as good as mine but the bunch of keys will do!

  68.

- **A source of music** - that you can turn on and off at will.
  71.

- **A large collection of newspaper cuttings** - story subject matter length and complexity selected according to the age and abilities of the group.
  75.

- **A powerful torch or spotlight.**
  83.

- **Cardboard boxes** - a number of various sizes.
  83.

- **A rolled up newspaper** - taped to keep it rolled up.
  85.

- **A collection of pictures of groups of people** - photographs, paintings or newspaper cuttings a minimum of six pictures per game.
  89.

- **A ring** - a curtain ring or similar.
  102.

- **A ball of string.**
  102.

- **A cup or mug** - preferably unbreakable and filled with water.
  103.

- **Small self-adhesive stickers** - sheets of various shapes, sizes and colours.
  114.

- **A numbered list of towns** - mounted on card and made durable. Make sure there are more towns on the list than the number of players likely to be in any group you work with.

  115.

- **Animal Cards** - a set of cards each one with the picture of an animal or name of an animal written on it. Each animal must be represented twice so that players can pair up.

  126.

- **Sound effects disc or tape** - thunder and rain.

  126v.

- **Coloured bands** - of the type used for sports two different colours one for each player in the two teams.

  127v.

- **A coin** - or similar token about the size of a fifty pence piece.

  129.

- **A large jar full of dried peas** - or similar objects. You will need at least two hundred of these (peas, not jars!).

  135.

Index

1.   AAARGH!!

This is a game of enormous fun that can be very noisy at times, especially if you are playing the variation - so it would be wise to ensure you will not disturb anyone else unduly when you are playing it. As well as being fun, it requires a considerable degree of concentration because our use of language is second nature and it is all too easy to overlook words relevant to the game. Furthermore, it lends itself to a high degree of sophistication and invention.

Equipment

- A chair for each Player.

Setting up

1. Sit everyone in a circle.
2. Choose a Starter.
3. Indicate the direction of play.

Playing

1. The Starter begins to tell a story. When the Starter gets to a word that indicates a sound (onomatopoeic or otherwise) the Starter must imitate the sound rather than say the word.

2. The story passes to the next Player and when that Player gets to the next word that indicates a sound he/she must imitate that sound. The story then passes to the next Player and so on around the circle.

Variations

1. Instead of just the Player who is telling the story making the sound everyone in the circle must join in.

2.   A.B.C.

There are two levels to this game. The first, in which the nonsense word or words are created requires a degree of co-operation amongst members of the group in order to arrange the letters in a satisfactory fashion. This co-operative effort is then used by each member of the group to make their own contribution to the ongoing story. And although the format is simple, it can lead to extremely complex and rich results.

Equipment

- A chair for each Player.
- A set (or several sets) of Alphabet Cards.

Setting up

1. Sit everyone in a circle.
2. Shuffle the cards well and place them face down on the floor in two piles, consonants and vowels.

Playing

1. Choose X number of Players to pick a consonant card each and Y number of Players to pick a vowel card each. The precise number of each depends on the size of the group and the size of the words you wish to create.

2. Ask the Players to arrange the letters into a nonsense word.

3. Use this nonsense word as the central object of an improvised story to which each member of the group contributes in turn (See also *STORY TIME*).

4. If the story requires more nonsense words create them in the same way.

Variations

1. Instead of telling a story create four or five words in the fashion described and tell the groups to use them as the basis for an improvisation.

3. ADDAROUND

A game requiring considerable concentration and some physical dexterity. As well as being fun in its own right it makes a very good physical warm up for further work - especially mime.

Equipment

- A chair for each Player.

Setting up

1. Sit everyone in a circle.
2. Choose a Starter.
3. Indicate the direction of play.

Playing

1. The Starter makes a simple movement.
   + *EXAMPLE: Scratching nose.*

2. The next Player repeats that movement and then adds one of their own.
   + *EXAMPLE: Scratching nose and waggling fingers.*

3. Each Player in turn repeats all the previous movements and then adds one of their own.
   + *EXAMPLE: Scratching nose, waggling fingers and turning head to the right.*

4. Anyone who forgets the sequence or muddles a movement is out.

5. When someone is out the game starts again with the next Player.

3. ADDAROUND

Variations

1. Instead of starting again with the next Player the game continues with the next Player.   The contribution of each Player who has been eliminated must be removed from the sequence.

2. Impose a rule of silence.

3. If the group is small increase the complexity of actions each Player must make.

4. ADVERB GAME

Although this is a well known and much played game it continues to fulfil a useful function as it is one of the best games in which language skills can be translated into action at one and the same time as reinforcing those same skills.

Equipment

- A chair for each Player.
- A pencil and a piece of paper for each Player.
- 2 boxes to draw the papers from.

Setting up

1. Split the group into two teams of equal size and sit the Players in two lines facing each other.
2. Distribute the paper and pencils.
3. Each Player must write an adverb on their piece of paper and then place the paper in their own team's box.
4. Swap the boxes.

Playing

1. One Player from each team takes a piece of paper from their new box, memorises the adverb and then faces their own team.

2. The members of the team have to work out what that adverb is. They do this by asking the Player to mime various actions like sleep, eat, pluck a chicken, in the way that the adverb qualifies.
   + *EXAMPLE: Sleep angrily, eat angrily, pluck a chicken angrily.*

3. When everyone has had a turn count up the number of correct guesses. The team with the most is the winner.

4. ADVERB GAME

Variations

1. If the group is small provide the adverbs for the Players and use the game as an exercise in miming skills instead of a competition.

2. Set a time limit for each adverb to be discovered.

3. Set a limit on the number of guesses to be made by the team or group.

LIST OF ADVERBS
Slowly
Quickly
Gently
Roughly
Carefully
Carelessly
Artistically
Thoughtfully
Haughtily
Blindly
Deftly
Weakly
Strongly
Haltingly
Reluctantly
Eagerly
Timidly
Aggressively

5. ADVERTS

Somewhere on the borderline of game and improvisation, this activity has the best of both worlds. Once again, there are two levels. The more creative the initial suggestions for products, the better the possibilities for advertising them.

Equipment

- A chair for each Player.
- A pencil and a piece of paper for each Player.
- A box from which the papers can be drawn.

Setting up

1. Sit everyone down and distribute the pencils and paper.
2. Get everyone to write the name of an imaginary product on their piece of paper.

   + *EXAMPLE: Ant Soup, Chocolate Flavoured Soap, Upside Down Cakes.*
3. Everyone folds their paper and places it in the box.
4. Split the group into smaller groups of three or four.

Playing

1. One Player from each group takes a piece of paper from the box.

2. All working at the same time each group has a set time to produce a polished television advertisement for the product that was chosen.

Variations

1. Repeat the process until all the products have been advertised.

2. As the group gets used to the exercise reduce the time allowed for improvisation.

6.   ALPHABET CLAP

A deceptively simple sounding game, this can be quite difficult to play. Early rounds of the game should be played to a slow rhythm as the rhythm itself can become mesmerising, making it difficult to concentrate on the real object of the game. Once players are confident about the game, it can be speeded up and played extremly quickly.

Equipment

* A chair for each Player.

Setting up

1. Sit everyone in a circle.
2. Choose a Starter.
3. Indicate the direction of play.

Playing

1. The Starter establishes the following rhythm based on a four beat cycle the whole cycle lasting about two seconds each beat of equal duration:-
    (a)   Clap thighs with both hands.
    (b)   Clap thighs with both hands.
    (c)   Clap thighs with both hands.
    (d)   Click fingers.
   Everything happens on the fourth beat.

2. Once the rhythm is established the Starter, on the fourth beat, calls out the name of any one letter of the alphabet.
   + *EXAMPLE:* **S.**

3. The next Player on the next two successive fourth beats calls out a word beginning with that letter plus a new letter.
   + *EXAMPLE:* **S**ugar *..... and the letter* **M.**

4.   This continues around the circle until someone misses a beat, cannot think of a word, or generally makes a mess of things.

   + *EXAMPLE:* **M**other ..... *and the letter* **Q**.

   Queen ...... *and the letter* **Z**.

   Zulu .... *and the letter* **B**.

5.   The game starts again with the next Player.

Variations

1.   Vary the speed of the rhythm to suit the group and the experience of its members.

2.   Each word can only be used once and anyone who repeats a word is out.

7. ALPHABETICAL SENTENCES

Some patience is required for this game and it is, perhaps, best suited to older players. Even then it is very rare for a sentence to be completed, let alone make any sort of real sense. As with many such exercises, however, the end product can often posses a logic and beauty of its own.

Equipment

- A chair for each Player.

Setting up

1. Sit everyone in a circle.
2. Choose a Starter.
3. Indicate the direction of play.

Playing

1. The Starter starts a sentence beginning with a word that starts with the letter A.

2. The next Player adds a word beginning with the letter B.

3. This continues until a twenty-six word sentence has been composed each successive word beginning with the next letter of the alphabet.
   + *EXAMPLE:* ***A Boy Can Do Everything For Gold, However I Just Know Little Michael Needs Other People's Qualities Regarding Special Training Under Very Wearying Xenophobic Yeomanly Zealots.***

4. Anyone who cannot think of a word to continue the sentence is out and the next Player takes up the challenge.

7.   ALPHABETICAL SENTENCES

Variations

1. Each Player is asked to add two words at a time each with a successive letter of the alphabet.
    + *EXAMPLE: Starter:*   *Aaron beautifully*
    Player 1: curled dogs
    Player 2: ears for
    Player 3: games however
    Player 4: interesting jealousy
    . . . . and so on.

2. Each Player is asked to add two words both starting with the same letter of the alphabet.
    + *EXAMPLE: Starter:*   *Aaron artfully*
    Player 1: borrowed bongos
    Player 2: caringly carried
    Player 3: darted downstairs
    Player 4: entertaining everyone
    . . . . and so on.

3. Each Player is asked to add three or more words at a time with successive letters of the alphabet or three or more words starting with the same letter.

4. Be mean and insist that the sentence makes sense.

8.   AT THE PARTY

If you are working with a group that has recently come together this can be a useful ice-breaker. Getting to know people can be extremely stressful and that stress acts as an inhibitor. Making a game of it often produces better results than formal introductions.

Equipment

- A chair for each Player.

Setting up

1. Sit everyone in a circle.
2. Get all the Players to give themselves a fictional name, age, address, occupation, hobbies, and so on. The list can be as long or as short as you want.
3. Give everyone a few moments to fix all these details in their own mind.

Playing

1. All the Players must get up and introduce themselves to as many people as possible taking in as much information as they can.

2. After a pre-set time sit everyone down and verbally test to see how much they have all remembered about each Player.

Variations

1. Set up a situation in which the Players are meeting. This will set limits to what they create.
   + *EXAMPLE: Delegates at a Trade Conference, at the Olympic Games.*

2. This can be used equally well with a group of strangers using their real identities and details.

9.   BALLOON DEBATE

One of the more intellectual games in this collection, debates of this sort have been used as entertainment for a very long time. One of the greatest strengths of the game is that it can be played at many levels.

Equipment

- A chair for each Player.
- Occupation Cards.

Setting up

1. Shuffle the cards and deal them one to each Player face down.
2. Each Player memorises their occupation.
3. All cards are returned.
4. Split the group into smaller groups of four.

Playing

1. Each four is a group of passengers in the basket of a balloon that is falling slowly but surely into shark-infested waters. The balloon will only carry one Player to safety. Each Player must argue for survival on the merits of their importance to society in the roles they have been given. This argument takes place in front of all the others who then vote on who should survive.

2. The survivors from each group of four are put into a balloon and the process repeated until only one Player is left.

Variations

1. Allow each member of the group to choose their occupation or position in society for themselves.

2. You can, of course, conduct a traditional balloon debate with the passengers choosing actual characters from history and the present day, researching them thoroughly and then debating their merits in front of an audience who may question these characters before being allowed to vote on who they believe should survive.

LIST OF CHARACTERS

Cleopatra

Julius Caesar

Abraham Lincoln

Florence Nightingale

William Shakespeare

Leonardo Da Vinci

Picasso

Joan of Arc

Napoleon

Boudicca

Socrates

Einstein

Mozart

Marie Curie

Nelson Mandela

Margaret Thatcher

Hitler

Winston Churchill

George Washington

Ghandi

Scott of the Arctic

Queen Elizabeth I

Yuri Gagarin

Galileo

Marie Antoinette

Nietzsche

Edison

10.   BEAT THE CIRCLE

With so many variations this can be played time and time again without players becoming bored. It is also requires a certain degree of physical dexterity as the ball can easily be dropped. If this is a problem, a more suitable object can be used for that particular group.

Equipment

- A chair for each Player.
- An object to pass around the circle - a tennis ball is ideal.

Setting up

1. Choose a Volunteer.
2. Sit everyone in a circle with the Volunteer in the middle.
3. Choose a Starter and give the Starter the object to be passed.

Playing

1. The Volunteer in the middle closes their eyes.

2. The Starter, choosing the direction of play, passes the object to the Player seated to the left or right who then passes it to the next Player and so on around the circle.

3. While the object is being passed round the Volunteer in the middle waits and when he/she feels ready then says **Stop.**

4. Whoever is in possession of the object when the Volunteer in the middle says **Stop** is the Player who has to beat the circle.

5. The object must now be passed around the circle from Player to Player as quickly as possible.

6.   In the time it takes for the object to complete one circuit the Player caught with the object must name six objects beginning with the letter A.

7.   If a Player succeeds he/she stays in the circle. Any Player who fails to beat the circle must swap places with the Player in the centre.

8.   Then the game begins again and this time the named objects must begin with the letter B.

Variations

1.   Alter the number of objects to be named. This will, to some extent, be determined by the size and capabilities of the group.

2.   Change the category of things to be named. Instead of nouns try adjectives or verbs.

3.   You may even want to have specific categories.
     + *EXAMPLE: Boys names or famous people.*

11.   BUILDING A SENTENCE

This game can move very quickly and produce some amazing and convoluted sentences. It is an extremely useful exercise for groups whose abilities to create complex sentences is limited because players have time to consider where they will take the sentence as well as having fun with it.

Equipment

- A chair for each Player.

Setting up

1. Sit everyone in a circle.
2. Choose a Starter.
3. Indicate the direction of play.

Playing

1. The Starter chooses a word to start a sentence and says it out loud.

2. The next Player repeats the word and adds one of their own.

3. This continues around the circle with each Player adding a word of their own after repeating all the previous ones.
   + *EXAMPLE: I. I can. I can run. I can run a. I can run a long. I can run a long way . . . . . and so on.*

4. If anyone misses a word, forgets, or cannot continue the sentence (which may well go on for a long time) then that person is out. The game starts again with the next Player.

Variations

1. Each Player adds two (or more) words at a time to the sentence.

An extremly simple and silly game which nonetheless requires a great deal of concentration.

Equipment

- A chair for each Player.

Setting up

1. Sit everyone in a circle.
2. Choose a Starter.

Playing

1. The game begins with the Starter and the two Players on either side of the Starter placing their hands in the air (as shown in the diagram) and wiggling their fingers.

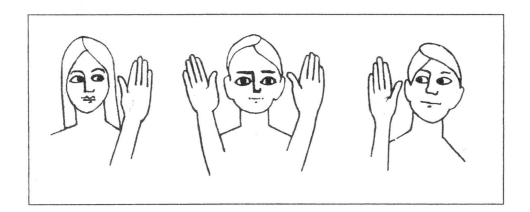

2. Once this is established the Starter drops both hands to their lap and the Players on either side do likewise following the Starter's lead. The Starter, however, must first clap both hands together and point them at somebody else in the circle.

3.   The Player pointed at together with the two Players on either side must then copy the action by holding their hands up in the air and wiggling their fingers.

4.   This continues back and forth across the circle slowly gathering speed. A Player must not point at the Player who has just pointed at them or at neighbouring Players seated on either side of them.

5.   When the game breaks down simply start again.

Variations

1.   Try it with more than one Starter so that several Bunnies are running at once.

13.   CAPTAIN'S SHIP

This game can be hard work to begin with. It takes a lot of setting up and players have to be familiar with all the calls and responses. However, once it has been played a few times, the rules and actions become second nature. That is when it comes into its own as a rowdy and energetic way to have fun. It can be played with enormous groups out of doors and is an excellent way of tiring people out.

Equipment

- A chair or dais for the Captain to stand on.
- A piece of chalk or masking tape.

Setting up

1. Clear the room of all obstacles.
2. Mark out on the floor the largest rectangle possible in the space available. If you have access to gymnasium mats or a large carpet then so much the better. This rectangle is the ship.
3. Choose a Volunteer. This is your Captain.
4. Spread everyone else out within the boundaries of the marked area. They are the Crew.
5. The Captain stands on the chair or dais at the bow of the ship.

Playing

1. The Captain calls out any one of a predetermined set of orders.

2. The Crew members all respond with a predetermined action.

3. The member of the Crew who is slowest in responding to each order or anyone who responds incorrectly is told to leave the ship and is eliminated.

4.   The Captain continues to call out orders until there is only one member of the Crew left. That player becomes the next Captain and the game starts again.

ORDERS	RESPONSES
Bow	All move to the bow.
Stern	All move to the stern.
Port	All move to port.
Starboard	All move to starboard.
Boom	All fall flat on faces.
Pirates	All take up positions of defence at the edges of the ship.
Captain	All salute.
Scrub decks	All on hands and knees scrubbing.
Lighthouse	All pirouette with arms outstretched.

Variations

1.   Increase the number of orders on the list to make the game more complex.

2.   Change the place in which the game occurs (and the type of orders and responses of course).

+ *EXAMPLE: Aboard a spaceship or inside a magic castle.*

14. CAT AND MOUSE

Essentially a chase game, this has sufficient complexities and variations built into it to make it that little bit more interesting.

Equipment

- A chair for each Player.
- A piece of cheese. This must be something that can be held easily in one hand but which will be heard when dropped. A small block of wood is ideal.

Setting up

1. Place the chairs in a circle and then discard one. Make sure that each chair is separated from those on either side by at least one chair's width.
2. Choose a Volunteer. This is the Mouse.
3. Sit everyone else in the circle. They are the Cats.
4. Give the piece of cheese to the Mouse.

Playing

1. The Mouse walks around the outside of the circle.

2. The Cats must face inwards toward the centre of the circle and keep their ears open.

3. On its travels around the outside of the circle the Mouse drops the cheese behind any one of the Cats that it chooses. The Mouse then starts to run around the outside of the circle.

4. On hearing the cheese hitting the floor directly behind it the Cat must get up, retrieve the cheese and then chase the Mouse.

5. The Mouse must attempt to reach the vacant chair and sit down. If the Mouse does this it is safe and the pursuing Cat now becomes a Mouse and the game starts again.

6. If the Cat catches the Mouse before it has a chance to sit down then the Cat returns to its seat and the Mouse must try again.

Variations

1. Use an object that rolls or bounces (such as a tennis ball) for the piece of cheese. This is also quieter than a block of wood so the Cats must listen all the more carefully.

2. Increase the number of circuits to be made before the Mouse can sit down.

3. If a Mouse is caught it is eliminated from the game but has the privilege of choosing the next Mouse (anyone but the Cat that caught it). Every time a Mouse is eliminated another chair is removed from the circle and the game begins again.

15.   CAUGHT NAPPING

Be prepared for mayhem. Inexperienced players are likely to make endless mistakes and may get a little frustrated with the game. If you persevere, however, they will get the hang of it. You will then need a sharp eye to act as referee as it can be played extremely quickly.

Equipment

- A chair for each Player.

Setting up

1. Sit everyone in a circle. Make the circle as large as possible.
2. Number everyone from one to however many there are.

Playing

1. On your command Player 1 calls out his/her own number and then somebody else's. Player 1 must then leave his/her chair and run to the chair of the Player whose number he/she has just called.
   + *EXAMPLE: Player 1. One . . . . . Seven.*

     Player 1 runs to Player 7's chair.

2. That Player needs to have said his/her own number, somebody else's number, have left his/her chair and be running to the chair of the Player whose number he/she has just called before Player 1 gets to their chair.
   + *EXAMPLE: Player 7. Seven . . . . . Eleven.*

     Player 7 then runs to Player 11's chair as Player 1 makes for Player 7's chair.

3. The game continues in this fashion until someone makes a mistake.

4. A Player cannot call out the number of the previous Player who has just called their number and is heading for their chair.

5. If a Player moves before saying his/her own number and somebody else's, or fails to do this before the Player who called their number arrives at their chair, or calls the number of someone who is already out of the game, or muddles numbers and fails to say them correctly then that Player is out of the game.

6. When someone is out, the game starts again with the last Player to move or whoever has the lowest number.

Variations

1. If the room in which you are playing is small ask Players to walk instead of running between the chairs.

2. For more advanced Players try playing the game carefully with everyone blindfolded.

3. Use letters of the alphabet or words instead of numbers.

16. CHAIN REACTION

As with some other games, this takes a bit of getting used to but once players get the hang of it, it will proceed at a great rate of knots.

Equipment

- None.

Setting up

1. Clear the room of all obstacles.
2. Put everyone into Pairs.
3. Choose a Volunteer Pair.

Playing

1. Pairs place themselves about the room at random. Then the partners of each Pair turn to face each other leaving a space of about 1 metre between them.

2. The two partners of the Volunteer Pair are named A and B.

3. On your command A begins to run in and out of the Pairs.

4. On your next command, giving A whatever lead you think proper, B starts to chase A following exactly the same route as A.

5. B must try to catch A.

6. A can avoid capture by splitting a Pair. This is done by standing between the two partners of a Pair. Then, whoever stands facing A's back must start to run. B must now chase that player.

7.   If A is caught by B before managing to split a Pair A must stay stationary until B has split a Pair. The chase then starts again with A chasing the new B.

Quick changes (that is the frequent splitting of Pairs) make for a more interesting game.

17.   CHANGES

After all the rushing about involved in some of the games this introduces a pleasant change of pace.   No rushing about and split second decision making - simply close observation. The more this game is played the more sophisticated it can become.

Equipment

*   None.

Setting up

1.   Choose a Volunteer.

Playing

1.   Everyone studies the room carefully.

2.   The Volunteer leaves the room.

3.   The rest of the group decide on a change to be made and an object is moved or hidden.

4.   The Volunteer returns to the room and has to spot the difference.

Variations

1.   Set a time limit for the Volunteer to discover the difference.

2.   Include the members of the group.
     + *EXAMPLE: Putting on or taking off a pair of glasses or swapping an item of clothing, a piece of jewellery or a watch.*

18.   CHANGE THE MIME

Another less energetic game that is useful for practising mime skills.

Equipment

* A chair for each Player.

Setting up

1. Sit everyone in a circle.
2. Choose a Starter.
3. Indicate the direction of play.
4. Impose a strict rule of silence.

Playing

1. The Starter stands in the middle of the circle and mimes an activity.
   + *EXAMPLE: Digging a hole.*

2. When the first Player understands what is being mimed the Player stands up, joins in and then alters the mime. The Starter then sits down.

3. This continues around the circle until each person has made a contribution.
   + *EXAMPLE: Digging a hole may become sweeping a floor which may become raking a lawn which may become pulling a trolley . . . . . and so on.*

Variations

1. Instead of each Player retiring as the next one takes over all the Players stay in the circle until everyone is involved in a final mime.

19. CHARADES

Another old favourite that has the distinction of being fun and also taxing the players.

Equipment

- A chair for each Player.
- A pencil and a piece of paper for each Player.
- 2 boxes for papers to be drawn from.

Setting up

1. Split the group into two teams.
2. Sit the Players in two lines facing each other.
3. Give everyone a pencil and a piece of paper.

Playing

1. Each Player writes the title of a film, book, album or track, play or television programme on their piece of paper.

2. The pieces of paper are placed in the boxes (one for each team) and then the boxes are swapped.

3. Each Player in turn takes a piece of paper from their own team's new box. After looking at what is written on the piece of paper the Player must mime the title to their own team.

4. The person who is miming has two minutes in which to perform.

5. If the Player's own team guesses the title correctly within the time limit the team gains a point. If they run out of time before getting the title, then the other team gains the point.

19.   CHARADES

Variations

1.   With a small group you can provide the titles and each person has a turn.

2.   Limit the titles to one medium such as films or television programmes.

LIST OF TITLES

Brief Encounter

One Flew Over the Cuckoo's Nest

Superman

The Lion King

Gone With the Wind

The Tempest

Midsummer Night's Dream

Twelfth Night

A Tale Of Two Cities

The Borrowers

The Importance Of Being Ernest

For Whom the Bell Tolls

What Katie Did

James and the Giant Peach

Three Men In a Boat

Hard Times

Much Ado About Nothing

Alice Through the Looking Glass

Wind In the Willows

Star Wars

Lord Of the Rings

War And Peace

The Ugly Duckling

Goldfinger

The Ten Commandments

The Thirty-Nine Steps

20.   CIRCLE OF DEATH

A good way of finishing a session with a group as it brings all the players together and ends with them all lying down and, if they are not convulsed with giggles, calm and quiet.

Equipment

- One chair.

Setting up

1.   Stand everyone in a circle with the chair just outside.

Playing

1.   On your command the Players begin to walk round in a circle.

2.   When you clap your hands everyone in the circle immediately stops moving. The Player who is beside the chair must then go to the centre of the circle and once there mime, in the most flamboyant of styles, a death scene.

3.   Repeat this until everyone is lying in a vast pile on the floor.

21.   CLAP-TRAP

This has always been a firm favourite with groups I have worked with. This is because it is easy to play but almost infinitely variable in the subjects that can be chosen.

Equipment

* A chair for each Player.

Setting up

1. Sit everyone in a circle.
2. Choose a Starter.
3. Indicate the direction of play.

Playing

1. The Starter establishes the following rhythm based on a four beat cycle the whole cycle lasting about two seconds each beat of equal duration:-
   (a)   Clap thighs with both hands.
   (b)   Clap thighs with both hands.
   (c)   Click fingers.
   (d)   Click fingers.
   Once the game has started everything must happen on the (c) and (d) beats when the finger clicking is happening.

2. Once the clap-clap-click-click rhythm is established, the Starter begins the game with the following phrase, **Names of - fa-mous** . . . - . . . choosing a category that will fit into the final two beats.
   + *EXAMPLE: Names of - fa-mous - **ath-letes** or Names of - fa-mous - **film stars**.*

3.   With the subject established, each Player, on their turn (that is, the next two finger click beats) must give a name that fits into the category chosen by the Starter.

+ *EXAMPLE: if the chosen category is film stars.*

> *1ˢᵗ Player: Tom Cruise*
>
> *2ⁿᵈ Player: Sean Penn . . . . . and so on.*

4.   Anyone who misses the correct beat, fails to name something, names incorrectly, or repeats something already said, is out and the game starts again with the next Player who chooses a new category.

Variations

1.   Start the game yourself a few times to establish a sensible speed to the rhythm. Once the group gets used to the game you can speed up the rhythm as much as you like.

22. COMMENTATOR'S BOX

It is difficult enough at the best of times having to describe a task to another person, particularly if it is one you know so well that it is second nature to you. The added complications here call for a considerable amount of imagination in the use of language.

Equipment

- A chair for each Player.

Setting up

1. Sit everyone in a circle.
2. Choose a Starter.

Playing

1. The Starter thinks of an action or a job (something very familiar to the Player).
   + *EXAMPLE: Writing a letter, changing a plug, saddling a horse.*

2. Having thought of something the Starter must then describe this action or job but is not allowed to mime any actions and should avoid using words that would give away what is being described.
   + *EXAMPLE: A description of writing a letter using a ball point pen might be:* **Pulling and pushing a small liquid filled tube with a tiny spherical apparatus housed in a cylindrical construction, with a conical addition at one end, across a flat surface.**

3. Whoever guesses correctly what the action or job is then has a turn at describing something.

23. COMPARISONS

Another game requiring imaginative use of language, this can have some quite hilarious results. It can also cut a bit close to the bone so it is important that members of the group know and trust one another.

Equipment

- A chair for each Player.

Setting up

1. Sit everyone in a circle.
2. Choose a Volunteer.

Playing

1. The Volunteer leaves the room.

2. The other Players choose an object in the room.

3. The Volunteer returns and tries to ascertain what object the rest of the group chose. The Volunteer does this by asking as many Players as necessary to provide information by pointing to a Player and saying, **"Compare it with me."**

4. The chosen Player must then make a comparison between the Volunteer and the object. The comparison can be far-fetched and inventive, a compliment or an insult, but it must have some connection with reality.
   + *EXAMPLE: If the object is a knife comparisons may be: hard as nails, sharp, useful, always around at meal times, ... and so on.*

5. When the Volunteer identifies the object the last Player to make a comparison goes out of the room and the game begins again.

24. CONCENTRATION

The name of this game is self-explanatory. The more players play it the more difficult you can make it, especially if you play the game on a regular basis. Like all skills, our ability to concentrate is increased the more we practice. This also makes a useful warm-up session for any sort of work that requires mental acuity.

Equipment

- A chair for each Player.

Setting up

1. Get everyone to take their chair and spread out in the room so that when they are sitting down each Player is as far away as possible from every other Player.

Playing

1. Ask everyone to close their eyes and in complete silence listen to sounds that are occurring outside the boundaries of the room.

2. Ask everyone to relax and tell you about what they heard.

3. Ask everyone to close their eyes and in complete silence listen for sounds occurring within the boundaries of the room.

4. Ask everyone to relax and tell you about what they heard.

5. Ask everyone to close their eyes and in complete silence listen to their own bodies.

Variations

1. Having established a routine of concentration ask everyone to close their eyes and in complete silence listen carefully. Once the Players are settled move around the room making a series of noises using objects that are part of the room. Ask everyone to relax and tell you what they heard, in the correct order, in what part of the room, with the number of steps that you took between each object.

   + *EXAMPLE: Opening and closing the door three times, walking ten paces to a lightswitch, switching the light off, walking six paces to a desk, screwing up a sheet of paper, throwing the paper into a bin.*

Equipment for variation 2

• A selection of objects that will produce interesting sounds.

2. Make noises with the objects not normally found in the room which were hidden from view when the group entered.

   + *EXAMPLE: Using a bicycle pump, blowing up a balloon and bursting the balloon, rattling and throwing down a number of pieces of cutlery, and so on.*

25. CONSEQUENCES PICTURE GAME

Younger players appreciate this game as it often leads to bizarre and hilarious finished pictures. The finished pictures can be used for storytelling or as the starting point of improvisational work.

Equipment

- A chair for each Player.
- A pencil and a piece of paper for each Player.

Setting up

1. Sit everyone in a circle.
2. Give everyone a pencil and a piece of paper.
3. Indicate the direction of play.

Playing

1. Each person draws the head and neck of a creature (as fabulous as they like) at the top of their piece of paper. When everyone has finished they fold the top of the paper over to hide what they have drawn leaving just enough showing for the next person to connect their part of the drawing.

2. All the papers are then passed on to the next Player. Each Player then draws the next section on the newly acquired sheet of paper, folding it over again when this section is completed, and passing it on as before.

3. This happens six times in all.

4. When the drawings are complete the Players unfold the pieces of paper and show the completed drawings to one another.

The sections of the drawing are:-

    (a)   Head and neck.

    (b)   Chest and upper arms.

    (c)   Abdomen and lower arms and hands.

    (d)   Upper legs.

    (e)   Lower legs.

    (f)   Feet.

+ *EXAMPLE:*

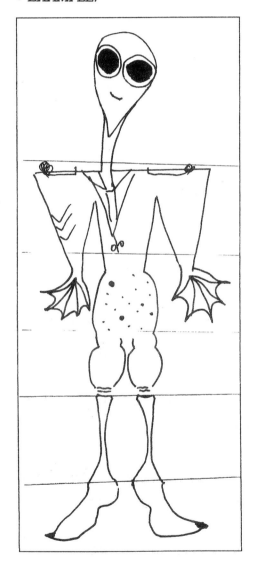 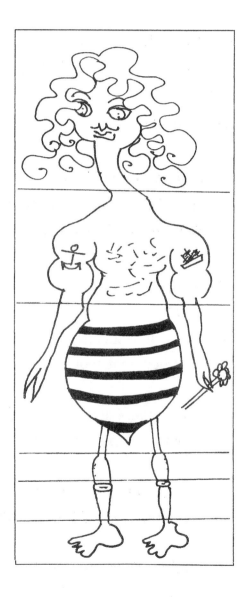

Variations

1.   The Players can be asked to draw something specific like clowns.

26. CONSEQUENCES WORD GAME

This more familiar form of consequences works better with older players whose skill with language is a little more advanced - sufficient for them to make a creative response to each of the commands. It is interesting to note the way in which players respond to certain aspects of this game. Their preoccupations can be most illuminating.

Equipment

- A chair for each Player.
- A pencil and a piece of paper for each Player.

Setting up

1. Sit everyone in a circle.
2. Give everyone a pencil and a piece of paper.
3. Indicate the direction of play.

Playing

1. On your instruction all the Players write down what they feel is an appropriate response to (a) at the top of their piece of paper.

2. The Players then fold the top of the paper over to hide what they have written and pass the paper on to the next Player.

3. Each Player then writes the next response to (b) at the top of their newly acquired piece of paper before folding it over and passing it on.

4. This continues until all eight responses have been made.

5. The finished papers are unfolded and read aloud.

26. CONSEQUENCES WORD GAME

The sequence of events to which Players are asked to respond:-

    (a)   She .....

    (b)   Met (a male) .....

    (c)   In or at .....

    (d)   She said .....

    (e)   He said .....

    (f)   So they .....

    (g)   And the consequence was .....

    (h)   The moral is .....

+ *EXAMPLE:* (a)   Madonna

    (b)   **Met** Donald Duck

    (c)   **At** a Turkish Bath

    (d)   **She said** "Can you tell me the time?."

    (e)   **He said** "I am not able to do that!"

    (f)   **So they** shared an egg mayonaise sandwich.

    (g)   **And the consequence was** they both had terrible indigestion.

    (h)   **The moral is** look before you leap.

Variations

1.   Take the game a step further by picking out the interesting finished pieces that make some sort of sense and using them as the basis for improvisation.

2.   Pick out those that don't make sense and use them as the basis for improvisation.

3.   Vary or increase the instructions to which Players respond.

27. COUPLES

Often dismissed as a party game, there is more to this game than breaking the ice. Apart from the obvious role in testing knowledge of pairs, there is the whole vexing question of identifying your 'natural' partner when you do not even know who you are yourself.

Equipment

- A set of Couples Cards.

Setting up

1. Stand everyone in a circle facing inwards.
2. Attach a card to the back of each person making sure that no one knows who they are.

Playing

1. On your command the circle breaks up and each Player tries to locate their other half.

2. Players may look at each others cards and talk to and ask questions of one another but no one is allowed to look at their own card or tell any other Player what is written on the card on their back.

Variations

1. Impose a time limit.

2. Only allow statements.

3. Allowing only questions with a Yes or No reply a Player continues to question the other until the answer is No when the turn ends and the other Player can either ask questions or move on.

28.   CREEP FOR THE KEYS

Silence is something that many people (and not just young ones) find difficult to maintain or cope with. Making a game of it is one step towards coping with it, as well as helping towards controlled movement.

Equipment

- A chair for each Player.
- A bunch of keys.

Setting up

1. Choose a Volunteer.
2. Sit everyone in a circle with the Volunteer in the middle.
3. Place the bunch of keys beneath the Volunteer's chair.
4. Impose a strict rule of silence.

Playing

1. The Volunteer closes his/her eyes.

2. Choose a Player at random and point to him/her. This is the Creeper.

3. The Creeper must leave his/her chair, creep up on the Volunteer, retrieve the keys and return to his/her own seat.

4. If a Creeper makes a noise the Volunteer opens his/her eyes and faces the Creeper. If a Creeper is caught in this way the Volunteer and Creeper change places and the game begins again.

5. If a Creeper succeeds in returning to his/her chair the Creeper rattles the keys. Then the Volunteer stays in the middle and the game starts again.

29. CREEPING VINE

Similar to the previous game *CREEP FOR THE KEYS* this is an old playground game that has gone under many a different name. The difference here is that everyone is moving at once which makes it much more difficult to achieve that all important element of silence.

Equipment

- None.

Setting up

1. Clear the room of all obstacles.
2. Choose a Volunteer.
3. The Volunteer stands at one end of the room facing the wall.
4. The rest of the group goes to the opposite end of the room facing the Volunteer.

Playing

1. On your command the group begins to approach the Volunteer who remains facing the wall.

2. If the Volunteer facing the wall hears a noise he/she can turn around.

3. If the Volunteer sees anyone moving whilst he/she is watching the Volunteer must name that person who is then sent back to the start.

4. When the Volunteer is satisfied that everyone else is still he/she turns back and faces the wall until hearing another noise.

5. The first person to reach and touch the Volunteer on the shoulder takes their place and the game starts again.

30.   DO THIS, DO THAT

A simple game of basic concentration. This is best played quickly and is useful as a filler if you have a few spare minutes or as one of a series of graded concentration exercises.

Equipment

* None.

Setting up

1. Choose a Leader.
2. Get everyone else to space themselves out in the room so they can all see the Leader clearly.

Playing

1. The Leader gives instructions to the group. Each instruction consists of the words, **Do this** followed by a demonstration of what the Leader wants done. Everyone in the group must obey.
    + *EXAMPLE: Raising both arms above the head, jumping up and down, or clapping hands and so on.*

2. At any time the Leader may give an instruction prefaced with the words, **Do that** followed by a demonstration.

3. Anyone in the group who obeys a **Do that** instruction is out.

4. The last person left becomes the next Leader.

31.   DO YOU LIKE YOUR NEIGHBOUR?

One of a number of seat swapping games, this can be noisy, chaotic, and great fun. It also requires a degree of concentration in order to react correctly to responses.

Equipment

- A chair for each Player.

Setting up

1. Choose a Volunteer.
2. Sit everyone in a circle with the Volunteer in the middle.

Playing

1. The object of the game is for the Volunteer to gain a seat in the circle by deposing another Player who must then take up the centre seat. The Volunteer does this by pointing to any Player he/she cares to choose in the circle and asking, **"Do you like your neighbour?"**

2. That person must immediately reply with either **Yes** or **No**. No other answer is acceptable.

3.   If the answer is **Yes** then the two Players on either side of the one questioned must stand up and swap seats as quickly as possible. While they are doing this the Volunteer in the middle may try to get to either of these two seats.

4. If the Volunteer is successful the deposed Player goes to the middle and the game starts again. If the Volunteer is unsuccessful he/she returns to the centre seat and tries again.

5.   If the person questioned answers **No** then everybody in the circle must get up and rush to a new seat. Once again the Volunteer in the middle tries to get to one of the seats in the circle.

6.   Whoever is left standing when all the seats in the circle are taken must go to the centre chair, point someone out and ask the question, **"Do you like your neighbour?"**

32. ELIMINATION

A mental detective game in which players soon learn to develop strategies for finding out what the hidden object might be.

Equipment

- A chair for each Player.

Setting up

1. Sit everyone in a circle.
2. Choose a Volunteer.

Playing

1. The Volunteer must think of an object (the more unusual the better).

2. Each Player in the circle is allowed to ask one question of the Volunteer in order to try and find out what object the Volunteer is thinking about.

3. The Volunteer is only allowed to answer either **Yes** or **No.**

4. By a process of elimination the Players in the group must try and work out the object the Volunteer is thinking about.

5. The Player who guesses correctly then has the privilege of thinking of the next object.

Variations

1. Allow Players more than one question each - especially if the group is small or play is sophisticated. (See Variation 2.)

2. Instead of a simple object like a box of matches the Volunteer can be very precise and as surreal as he/she likes.

+ *EXAMPLE: A twelve foot purple elephant with fluorescent green spots wearing diamond earrings, a top hat, two pairs of slippers and a sock on his trunk.*

3. Instead of an object the Volunteer should think of a real or fictional person as long as the Volunteer knows that person sufficiently well to answer detailed questions.

4. Instead of an object or person the Volunteer should think of an animal that is known sufficiently well for the Volunteer to answer detailed questions accurately.

LIST OF OBJECTS

A door key

A spiral staircase

A fork-lift truck

The Great Wall of China

The Eiffel Tower

A split pea

A gazebo

A funnel

A hub cap

A magician's wand

Trouser turn-ups

An apple pip

A buttonhole

A washer

A banana skin

A shoe lace

Sardine sandwiches

Welsh rarebit

Although the game has a simple formula, it soon becomes apparent that it is not easy to play for any length of time. Even players with large vocabularies can find themselves struggling.

Equipment

- A chair for each Player.

Setting up

1. Sit everyone in a circle.
2. Choose a Starter.
3. Indicate the direction of play.

Playing

1. The Starter calls out the first noun that comes into his/her head.
   + *EXAMPLE: Starter: Dog.*

2. The next Player must call out a noun that begins with the last letter of the previous word.
   + *EXAMPLE: Player 1: Goblin. (DoG - Goblin)*

3. This continues around the circle with each consecutive Player calling out a noun beginning with last letter of the previous word.
   + *EXAMPLE: Player 2: Nozzle. (GobliN - Nozzle)*
   Player 3: Elderberry. (Nozzle - Elderberry)
   Player 4: Yew. And so on.

4. Anyone who repeats a word, makes a mistake or cannot think of anything is out.

5. The game starts again with the next Player.

More overtly competitive than most of the games, in that score is kept, this game also borders on the edge of situational play. A great deal of concentration is required by players to manoeuvre with their eyes closed, stay oriented, and listen out for others.

Equipment

- A room with blackout and variable light control. This is not essential but very useful.

Setting up

1. Clear the room of all obstacles.
2. Split the group into four smaller groups - A, B, C and D.
3. Put groups B, C and D at one end of the room. They are the Escapees.
4. Put group A, about three-quarters of the room's length away from the others. They are the Guards.
5. Everyone closes their eyes and must keep them closed throughout the game.
6. If you do have blackout and light control reduce the light level to a minimum leaving enough for you to see and judge.
7. Impose a strict rule of silence with the exception of two words - **Guard** and **Caught** - which are used in the game.

Playing

1. The object of the game is for the Escapees to get from one end of the room to the other without being caught and for the Guards to catch as many Escapees as they can.

2. On your command the Escapees begin to move as quietly as they can from one end of the room to the other.

3. At the same time the Guards must try to locate Escapees by listening carefully and then capture the Escapees by touching them.

4. If a Guard touches someone they must both stop and the Guard must say **Guard.**

5. If the person the Guard caught is also a Guard then that person must respond by saying **Guard** to obtain his/her release.

6. If the person the Guard caught is an Escapee then that person must respond by saying **Caught** and open their eyes and return to the starting place without interfering with the game.

7. When all the Escapees are disposed of - either by being caught and returned to the start or by reaching freedom (the far wall) - count up the number of Escapees caught. This is the guarding team's score.

8. Repeat the game until every group has had a go at guarding. Compare scores.

35.   EYE WITNESS

Memory and concentration are put to the test here because not only must players watch others perform and later recall what they did, they must also remember their own improvisational roles. One thing that players will learn from this is that no matter how good they get at it and no matter how hard they concentrate, no one person will ever witness an event identically to any other person. There will always be discrepancies, no matter how small - something the police know very well from witness statements.

Equipment

- None.

Setting up

1.   Split the group into four or five Small Groups.

Playing

1.   The Small Groups are given a set time to organise a detailed improvisation in which an incident occurs. This can be anything as long as there is sufficient detail to set a challenge.

2.   At the end of the allotted time each Small Group shows their improvisation to the rest.

3.   When all the incidents have been shown go back to the first Small Group and with these group members acting as judges get the rest to give a detailed verbal account of everything that happened in the improvisation.

4.   Repeat this with each Small Group.

36. FEELY TIME

All too often **we** rely on several of our senses combined to help us interpret the world. Some games like *ESCAPE IN THE DARK* and *BUNNIES* rely entirely on the sole use of hearing or vision. Here, players are asked to use only their sense of touch to identify things and it can be quite disorientating to realise how difficult it can be to identify even the most commonplace and ordininary everyday objects.

Equipment

- A chair for each Player and one spare.
- A table.
- A Feely Box.
- A collection of objects to place in the Feely Box.

Setting up

1. Sit everyone facing the table.
2. Place the spare chair on the other side of the table.
3. Place the Feely Box on the table the open side facing the group.
4. Make sure the objects to be felt are in another box or inside a drawer and not visible to anyone.
5. Choose a Volunteer.

Playing

1. The Volunteer sits in the chair at the table and closes his/her eyes.

2. Place an object in the Feely Box.

3. When the object is in the Feely Box the Volunteer opens his/her eyes and then puts a hand through the small hole and feels the object.

4. The Volunteer is allowed several tries but a time limit is set in which the Volunteer must identify the object.

5. Repeat with the rest of the group using a different object for each Player.

Variations

1. Impose a strict rule of silence. The Volunteer is only allowed one try at identifying the object within the time limit.

2. Allow the group to help the Volunteer in a select and predetermined way by allowing the Volunteer to ask a person in the group to mime a clue demonstrating the object in use.
    + *EXAMPLE: If the object in the Feely Box is a toothbrush the mime could be brushing the teeth.*

3. Use the same object twice or more.

4. Use a selection of shiny, smooth hard objects like cutlery, a pebble, an apple or a mirror.

5. Use a selection of soft and rough objects like a marshmallow and a sheet of sandpaper.

6. Use flat or solid mathematical shapes.

7. Use plastic or card letters or numbers.

With some skilled playing, this game can go on for a long time with the poor volunteer stuck in the middle unable to identify the leader. However, if the volunteer is equally skilled, someone will sooner or later give the game away and looking for small tell-tale signs is what the game is all about.

Equipment

* A chair for each Player.

Setting up

1. Sit everyone in a circle.
2. Choose a Volunteer.
3. Send the Volunteer out of the room.
4. Choose a Leader.

Playing

1. The Leader performs a series of simple actions.
   + *EXAMPLE: Head scratching, finger flapping, toe tapping.*

2. The rest of the group must then copy the Leader's movements exactly.

3. Immediately everyone is active the Volunteer is brought back into the room and stands in the middle of the circle.

4. The Volunteer must try to identify the Leader and watches carefully as all the Players carry out their actions. The trick is for everyone in the group not to look at the Leader but for each Player to watch someone else who is watching someone who is watching the Leader.

5. When the Volunteer identifies the Leader, the Leader goes out of the room, a new Volounteer is chosen and the game starts again.

38.   FIND THE RABBIT

Although a degree of skill is required for this it is far outweighed by the fun.

Equipment

- A chair for each Player except the Volunteer.

Setting up

1. Choose a Volunteer.
2. Sit everyone else in a circle.

Playing

1. The Volunteer stands in the middle of the circle.

2. All the Players in the circle place their hands palm forwards at the sides of their head.

3. When the Volunteer is looking directly at anyone the Player must keep his/her hands perfectly still.

4. Anyone who cannot be seen by the Volunteer may waggle their fingers.

5. The Volunteer turns around quickly in either direction and must try to catch someone waggling their fingers.

6. The Volunteer swaps places with the first Player to be caught out and the game starts again.

There are not many games that genuinely exercise numerical skills. This is one of the few and an old favourite. It does require a certain level of numeracy on the part of the players (as well as yourself) but is nonetheless rewarding. It is not always those good at mathematics who excel in this sort of situation.

Equipment

* A chair for each Player.

Setting up

1. Sit everyone in a circle.
2. Choose a Starter.
3. Indicate the direction of play.
4. Choose the key number: (a) anything from 3 to 9 for averagely numerate groups.

    (b) 10 to 99 for very numerate and tolerant groups.

    (c) 1 or 2 for very numerate groups who want to play a very silly game.

Playing

1. The Starter starts counting by saying **One.**

2. The next Player says **Two,** the next Player says **Three** and so on.

3. Every time a number is reached in which the key number appears the Player must say **Fizz** instead of saying the number. So, if the key number is 7, it appears in 7, 17, 27, 37, 47, 57, 67, 70, 71, 72, and so on.

    + *EXAMPLE: One, two, three, four, five, six, **Fizz**, eight, nine, ten, eleven, twelve, thirteen, fourteen, fifteen, sixteen, **Fizz**, eighteen, and so on.*

4. Every time a number is reached that is a multiple of the key number the Player must say **Buzz** instead of the number. So, if the key number is 7, the multiples are 7, 14, 21, 28, 35, and so on.

+ *EXAMPLE: One, two, three, four, five, six, **Buzz**, eight, nine, ten, eleven, twelve, thirteen, **Buzz**, fifteen, sixteen, seventeen, eighteen, nineteen, twenty, **Buzz**, twenty-two, and so on.*

5. Every time a number is reached that is both a multiple of the key number and a number in which the key number appears the Player must say **Fizz-Buzz** instead of the number. So, if the key number is 7, the **Fizz-Buzz** numbers are 7, 70, 77, and so on.

+ *EXAMPLE: One, two, three, four, five six, **Fizz-Buzz**, eight, nine, ten, eleven, twelve, thirteen, fourteen, fifteen, sixteen, seventeen, eighteen, nineteen, twenty, twenty-one, twenty-two, and so on.*

6. Failure to get any of the **Fizzes**, **Buzzes** or **Fizz-Buzzes** correct results in elimination from the game. So, if the key number is 7, the numbers in the sequence that must be avoided are 7, 14, 17, 21, 27, 28, 35, 37, 42, 47, and so on.

+ *EXAMPLE: One, two, three, four, five, six, **Fizz-Buzz**, eight, nine, ten, eleven, twelve, thirteen, **Buzz**, fifteen, sixteen, **Fizz**, eighteen, nineteen, twenty, **Buzz**, twenty-two, twenty-three, twenty-four, twenty-five, twenty-six, **Fizz**, **Buzz**, twenty-nine, thirty, thirty-one, thirty-two, thirty-three, thirty-four, **Buzz**, thirty-six, **Fizz**, thirty-eight, thirty-nine, and so on.*

7. When a Player is out the game can either carry on with the next person continuing the sequence correctly or the game can start again with a new key number.

40. FORTUNATELY - UNFORTUNATELY

A degree of sophistication and inventiveness is required of players if this is not to become a somewhat tedious kicking back and forth. Good players, however, will be able to salvage and destroy the fortunes of characters in the most satisfying of ways.

Equipment

- A chair for each Player.

Setting up

1. Sit everyone in a circle.
2. Choose a Starter.
3. Indicate the direction of play.

Playing

1. The Starter tells the first sentence of a story prefacing the sentence with **Fortunately** . . . . .

2. The next Player continues the story prefacing their sentence with **Unfortunately** . . . . .

3. This continues around the circle with each alternate sentence starting **Fortunately / Unfortunately** and making reasonable sense within the context of the story. Players must avoid repetition or hesitation.

Variations

1. Allow each Player several sentences or allow a Player to continue with the story until you choose to move it on to the next person.

2. Allow each Player a set time.

41.   FOX AND RABBIT

This chase game requires a bit of setting up but if you have sufficient space it can be a fast and exciting game.   It can certainly exhaust the most energetic of players.

Equipment

* None.

Setting up

1.   Make the sure the room is clear of all obstacles.
2.   Choose two Volunteers.
3.   Divide the rest of the group into a minimum of five smaller groups.   If you have enough Players and the space more groups are acceptable.
4.   Arrange the small groups so that one Player from each forms a large circle with plenty of space between each Player.   They must all face into the centre of the circle.
5.   The rest of the members of each of the smaller groups line up behind their front member.   They must also face towards the centre of the circle.   When this is complete the groups will look like the spokes of a large wheel.
6.   The gaps between the lines are rabbit holes leading to the warren which is the space at the centre.
7.   Designate one of the Volunteers as the Fox and the other as the Rabbit.
8.   The Fox and Rabbit stand outside the circle of Players on opposite sides of the circle.

Playing

1.   On your command the Fox chases the Rabbit outside the circle.   They can chase anywhere outside the circle.

2.   The Rabbit reaches safety by entering a rabbit hole.   The Fox is not allowed to enter any of the rabbit holes.

3. Once in the warren the Rabbit must join the front of a line facing into the centre of the circle. The Player at the back of the line becomes the new Rabbit and must start to run.

4. If a Fox catches a Rabbit by touching it that Rabbit then becomes the next Fox.

5. The retiring Fox goes into the warren and joins the front of any line and the Player at the back of the line becomes the new Rabbit and the game starts again.

Variations

1. Impose a time period before any Rabbit can run for safety down a rabbit hole.

2. Block off some of the holes with chairs.

3. Have more than one Rabbit or more than one Fox at any one time.

42. FRUIT BOWL

More mayhem requiring a degree of concentration but played mostly for fun. Another useful game for tiring players out.

Equipment

- A chair for each Player.

Setting up

1. Choose a Volunteer.
2. Sit everyone in a circle with the Volunteer in the middle.
3. Name everyone including the Volunteer: Apple, Orange, Banana, Lemon. Apple, Orange, Banana, Lemon ..... and so on.

Playing

1. The Volunteer calls out the name of one of the four fruits.
   + *EXAMPLE: Orange.*

2. When Players in the circle hear the name of their fruit called out they must immediately stand up and run to another vacant chair. The Volunteer in the middle also stands up and tries to get to one of the vacant seats in the circle.

3. In addition to **Apple, Orange, Banana, Lemon** the Volunteer in the middle may also call out **Fruit Bowl**. If this happens everyone must stand up and run to another seat.

4. After the scramble for chairs the Player left standing must go to the middle and sit down and then the game begins again.

Variations

1. There are many names for this game and consequently names for the four items that can be called out.

    + *EXAMPLE: Frying Pan - Sausage, Bacon, Egg, Chips.*

                         Zoo - Zebra, Camel, Lion, Snake.

2. If you have a large group or wish to make the game more complicated increase the number of items to be called out.

    + *EXAMPLE: Fruit Bowl - Apple, Pear, Orange, Banana, Lemon, Grape, Cherry.*

43. FURNITURE GAME

A game that involves a little lateral thinking in order to identify a person by likening their characteristics to an object, an animal or an abstract.

Equipment

* A chair for each Player.

Setting up

1. Sit everyone in a circle.
2. Choose a Starter.

Playing

1. The Starter chooses another person in the group without telling anyone else who it is.

2. Each Player in turn moving clockwise from the Starter then asks the Starter **If this person were a . . . . . . what would they be?**

3. The first Player always asks **If this person were a piece of furniture what would they be?**

4. Thereafter each Player can ask what sort of animal, song, plant, car, or whatever other category any Player can think of.

5. The Starter must answer as accurately as possible.

6. When a Player thinks he/she knows who is being described he/she puts his/her hand up. If the guess is wrong the game continues. If the guess is right it is this Player's turn to think of someone else and the game begins again.

44. GOBBLEDEGOOK GUIDE

Speaking gobbledegook or gibberish (meaning nonsense language) can be extremely difficult and the players will require a degree of practice if what they say is not to sound somewhat weak in comparison with a genuine language. However, the real secret is not to try to be incredibly inventive with new sounds but to use the right tone of voice and give what is said the right inflection. It will soon become apparent that much of what we convey to one another is in the way we say it as much as in the content.

Equipment

- None.

Setting up

1. Put everyone into groups of four or thereabouts.
2. The Players name themselves A, B, C and D.

Playing

1. All the A Players come to you and you give them a location.
   + *EXAMPLE: A cathedral, a railway station, a boat.*

2. The A Players return to their groups and proceed to give them a guided tour of the location. The whole thing must be done in gobbledegook.

3. Whichever Player in the group guesses the location then becomes the new guide who thinks of a new location and proceeds to guide the group round it.

Variations

1. Instead of describing a location the guide must give instructions for an activity or commentate at an event in gobbledegook.

45.   GOING TO NEWPORT

A memory game with a difference, Newport becomes the scene of any number of activities involving all those objects taken there in the first place. There is much distraction along the way as players find themselves having to do the most inappropriate things to their chosen objects.

Equipment

- A chair for each Player

Setting up

1. Sit everyone in a circle.
2. Choose a Starter.
3. Indicate the direction of play.

Playing

ROUND 1

1. The Starter begins the game by saying **I am going to Newport and will take my . . . . .** naming whatever it is he/she wishes to take.

   + *EXAMPLE: Starter: I am going to Newport and will take my dog.*

2. This continues around the circle until each person has named one item which must be different from every other Player.

   + *EXAMPLE: Starter: I am going to Newport and will take my **dog**.*

   *Player 1: I am going to Newport and will take my **cream bun.***

   *Player 2: I am going to Newport and will take my **goldfish**.*

   *Player 3: I am going to Newport and will take my **trombone**.*

ROUND 2

3. Once each Player has named something the second round begins with the Starter telling the group what he/she is going to do with the item he/she has chosen to take. It must be something appropriate.

+ *EXAMPLE: The Starter may say* **In Newport I will wash my dog.**

4. This continues with each successive Player saying the phrase   **In Newport I will wash my . . . . .** adding whatever it is that the Player said he/she was going to take to Newport in the first round.

+ *EXAMPLE: Player 1 who chose to take a cream bun to Newport in the first round needs to say* **In Newport I will wash my cream bun.**

Player 2 who chose to take a goldfish to Newport needs to say **In Newport I will wash my goldfish.**

Player 3: **In Newport I will wash my trombone.**

And so on right around the circle.

ROUND 3

5. The Player sitting next to the Starter begins the third round by saying what he/she will do in Newport with his/her chosen object from the first round.

+ *EXAMPLE: Player 1* **In Newport I will eat my cream bun.**

Player 2 who chose a goldfish in the first round needs to say **In Newport I will eat my goldfish.**

Player 3 who chose a trombone in the first round needs to say **In Newport I will eat my trombone.**

And so on right around the circle.

6. This continues until everyone has had a go at starting a round or everyone is out from making a mess of things.

46. GROUPS

This game has much in common with *COUPLES* but it is better suited to larger groups. Although easier to play than *COUPLES* it can be made more difficult if you choose groups that have interchangeable members.

Equipment

- A set of Simple or Interchangeable Group Cards.
  + *EXAMPLE: Simple*   *(a) Red, Blue,Yellow*

                                       (b) Knife, Fork, Spoon.

      Interchangeable (a) **Diamonds**, *Emeralds, Pearls, Rubies.*

                            (b) Clubs, Spades, Hearts, **Diamonds***.*

Setting up

1. Stand everyone in a circle facing inwards.
2. Attach a card to the back of each Player making sure no one knows who or what they are.

Playing

1. On your command the circle breaks up and each Player tries to locate the other members of their group.

2. Players may talk to one another but no one is allowed to look at their own card or tell any other Player what is on the card on their back

Variations

1. Impose a time limit.

2. Allow only questions with **Yes** or **No** for an answer.

3. Allow only statements.

47. HAND MEMORY GAME

Another game involving the sense of touch. This time, however, texture is not a factor and the differences in shape that can be generated are quite small.

Equipment

• None.

Setting up

1. Split the group into two smaller groups of equal size.

2. Name one group of Players the A's and the other the B's.

Playing

1. A Players spread out and close their eyes.

2. B Players select a partner and stand in front of them.

3. All the B Players form their hands into a shape.

4. A Players with eyes closed feel their partner's hands.

5. B Players keeping their hands in those same shapes form a circle all facing outwards.

6. A Players must then open their eyes and try to identify their partners by looking at and feeling the hands of all the Players in the circle.

7. Reverse the roles and play again.

48. HAND TO FACE

This can be a real test of how well members of a group know one another. It also requires a degree of pre-existing trust for players to allow others to touch their faces.

Equipment

- None.

Setting up

1. Put everyone into pairs.
2. Each pair of Players name themselves A and B.
3. Impose a strict rule of silence.

Playing

1. The Pairs spread out in the room and the Players stand facing each other.

2. A Players close their eyes.

3. B Players move around and find themselves new partners.

4. All the A Players must now identify their new partners by carefully feeling their faces.

5. Reverse the roles and play again.

49.   I AM GOING TO NORWICH

Another game that seems simple but which places a lot of pressure on the player chosen. Thinking of three things beginning with the same letter in a short space of time is far from easy.

Equipment

- A chair for each Player.

Setting up

1. Sit everyone in a circle.
2. Choose a Volunteer.

Playing

1. The Volunteer stands in the middle points to any Player of his/her choice and says **I am going to** ..... adding the name of any town he/she wants. Having done that the Volunteer starts to count to ten out loud.
   + *EXAMPLE: Volunteer: I am going to **Norwich**.*

2. Whilst the Volunteer is counting to ten the Player pointed to must call out the names of three things beginning with the same letter as the first letter of the town.
   + *EXAMPLE: Player: **N**asturtium, **N**ets, **N**otebook.*

3. If a Player succeeds he/she stays put and the Volunteer points to someone else and tries again with a different town.

4. If a Player fails he/she swaps places with the Volunteer and the game starts again.

49.   I AM GOING TO NORWICH

Variations

1. Provide a list of towns if Players have an uncertain knowledge of names.

2. Provide a list of names of countries, capital cities or rivers beginning with a different letter of the alphabet and use this instead for a change.

LIST OF TOWNS AND CITIES	LIST OF COUNTRIES AND REGIONS
Adelaide	Argentina
Belfast	Belgium
Calgary	Canada
Dover	Denmark
Eden	England
Florence	France
Gloucester	Guyana
Hamilton	Holland
Islamabad	Iceland
Jacksonville	Jamaica
Kingston	Kenya
London	Libya
Manchester	Mexico
New York	Norway
Oxford	Oman
Penang	Portugal
Queenstown	Qatar
Rotterdam	Russia
Sienna	Sweden
Toronto	Turkey
Upton	United States of America
Valencia	Venezuela
Whitby	Wales
Xenia	Xadeed
York	Yalta
Zanzibar	Zambia

50.   IF WISHES WERE HORSES

A variant guessing game that has the added difficulty of dealing with more abstract notions.   Working out the identity of an object by process of elimination lends itself to certain strategies that are not available to the players in this case.

Equipment

- A chair for each Player.

Setting up

1.   Choose a Volunteer.
2.   Sit everyone in a semi-circle facing the Volunteer.

Playing

1.   The Volunteer thinks of a wish that he/she would like fulfilled.

2.   The other Players must attempt to work out what the wish is. They do this by questioning the Volunteer who can only answer **Yes** or **No**.

3.   When enough information has been elicited a Player may make a guess at what the wish is. If the guess is correct the Player has a turn at making a wish. If the guess is wrong the Player is out of the game for that round.

Variations

1.   Set a time limit.

2.   Set a limit to the number of questions that can be asked by the group or by individuals.

51.   I LOVE MY LOVE

As with all such games as this, the exercise of vocabulary is important but should never be the prime concern otherwise it becomes a dull exercise.

Equipment

- A chair for each Player.

Setting up

1. Sit everyone in a circle.
2. Choose a Starter.
3. Indicate the direction of play.

Playing

1. The Starter begins the game by saying **I love my love with an A because she/he is ......** adding an adjective beginning with A.
   + *EXAMPLE: I love my love with an **A** because he is **A**ustere.*

2. The next Player continues by saying **I love my love with a B because she/he is ..... adding an adjective beginning with a B.**
   + *EXAMPLE: I love my love with an **B** because she is **B**lameless.*

3. This continues around the circle working through the entire alphabet.

4. Anyone who makes a mistake or cannot think of an appropriate adjective is out and the game continues with the next Player.

Equipment for Variation 1

- Alphabet Cards.

Variations

1. Using a set of well-shuffled Alphabet Cards indicate what the letter is to be at the time each Player takes his/her turn to prevent any of the Players having an advantage over others by having plenty of time to think of an adjective.

2. Players must stick to one letter of the alphabet for a whole round.

3. Allow invented adjectives to be used.
   + *EXAMPLE: I love my love with an **A** because she is **A**usplendiferous.*

4. Various formulae can be introduced so that each Player may have to supply a variety of additional information like I love my love with an A because her/his name is . . . . . she/he lives in . . . . . and she/he is . . . . .
   + *EXAMPLE: I love my love with an **A** because her name is **A**nastasia she lives in **A**berdeen and she is **A**mazing.*
   *I love my love with an **A** because his name is **A**lan he lives in **A**scot and he is **A**ssertive.*

Even though players are familiar with their own initials this game can prove to be a real brain twister. If you play it a lot then players will rehearse answers so it is wise to keep ahead of them and invent as many unusual categories as you can. This is a game that can be played on car journeys, using the letters of car registration plates instead of players initials.

Equipment

- A chair for each Player.

Setting up

1. Sit everyone in a circle.
2. Choose a Starter.
3. Indicate the direction of play.

Playing

1. Nominate a category.

    + *EXAMPLE: Hobbies, In My Shopping Basket or Holidays.*

2. Each Player in turn must make up a two word answer to fit that category based on the initials of their first and last names.

    + *EXAMPLE: If you give **Hobbies** as the category - **G**loria **B**arnes might say **G**arden **B**owls, **J**ohn **W**ilkes might say **J**oined-up **W**riting and **C**atherine **F**letcher might say **C**atching **F**ish.*
    *A different category such as **In My Shopping Basket** might get the following answers: **G**reen **B**ananas, **J**ammy **W**afers and **C**anned **F**ruit.*

3. Anyone who makes a mistake or cannot think of something or whose answer is too absurd or just generally messes up is out for that round.

Based on a party game in which all the answers are written down, this has the added fun of not knowing which letter will turn up next.

Equipment

- A chair for each Player.
- A set of Alphabet Cards.

Setting up

1. Sit everyone in a circle.
2. Choose a Volunteer.
3. Choose a Starter.
4. Indicate the direction of play.

Playing

1. The Volunteer is given the set of well shuffled Alphabet Cards and stands in the centre of the circle.

2. A category is chosen.
   + *EXAMPLE: Flowers, Cities, Names, and so on.*

3. The Volunteer turns up the first card in the pack and calls out the letter on it. The Starter must name something in the chosen category beginning with that letter.
   + *EXAMPLE: If the chosen category is **Flowers** and the letter is **I** the answer might be **Iris**.*

4. The next card is turned up and the next Player names something in the same category beginning with the letter on this card.
   + *EXAMPLE: The chosen category is **Flowers** and the letter on the next card is **D** the answer might be **Daffodil**.*

5.   This continues around the circle. Anyone who hesitates or calls out something inappropriate to the category or just generally messes up is out. The game continues with the next Player.

6.   Once the game has gone around the circle once the cards are shuffled a new category is chosen and the game resumes.

7.   The last Player left is the winner.

LIST OF FLOWERS

(Remove the U from the pack of Alphabet Cards.)

Agapanthus

Bird of Paradise Flower

Calla Lily

Delphinium

Euphorbia

Freesia

Gerbera

Hydrangea

Iris

Knapweed

Larkspur

Muscari

Nigella

Orchid

Peony

Quince flower

Rose

Snapdragon

Tulip

Veronica

Waxflower

Yarrow

Zantedschia

54. INSTRUCTIONS

The increasing complexity of this game is what takes the toll of players. Even so, it is surprising just how much players are capable of remembering. Furthermore, practice increases this capacity.

Equipment

* A chair for each Player.

Setting up

1. Sit everyone in a circle.
2. Choose a Starter.

Playing

1. The Starter gives an instruction. Everybody else obeys.

2. The Starter gives two instructions. Everybody else obeys.

3. The Starter gives three instructions, then four, then five, and so on. Each time the other Players obey the instructions.

4. If a Player fails to obey the instructions correctly, mixes the order, misses something out or generally makes a mess of things the Player is out.

5. The last Player left becomes the next Starter.

55.   IN THE DARK

Trust in others and reliance on a limited set of senses may make this a difficult game to carry out to begin with. Many players will be hesitant. However, as a group gains confidence, these tasks can be carried out quickly and without mishap. The game also makes a useful warm up for group work.

Equipment

- A chair for each Player.

Setting up

1. Put everyone into pairs.
2. The Players name themselves A and B.
3. Impose a strict rule of silence.

Playing

1. A Players take their chairs and sit randomly about the room. They close their eyes.

2. All the B Players place their chairs at random a distance away from their partners in some other part of the room.

3. B Players using only hand contact must guide their partners around all the obstacles of chairs and moving people from one chair to the other.

4. Reverse roles and play again.

Variations

1. Instead of continuous hand contact reduce it to a set of tactile instructions.

55. IN THE DARK

INSTRUCTIONS	RESPONSES
Tap partner's left shoulder	Move left.
Tap partner's right shoulder	Move right.
Tap between partner's shoulders	Stop.
Tap top of partner's head	Move forward.

56.   IN THE DARK AGAIN

This variant of the previous game is much more difficult to play. Given the problems already outlined, they are compounded here by the fact that guidance comes from afar and has to be picked out from all the other instructions being called out. Chaos is likely to reign to begin with, but if players persevere they will soon learn to concentrate on the one voice they need to hear.

Equipment

- A chair for each Player.

Setting up

1. Put everyone into pairs.
2. The Players name themselves A and B.

Playing

1. A Players take their chairs and sit randomly about the room. They close their eyes.

2. All the B Players place their chairs at random a distance away from their partners in some other part of the room.

3. The B Players using only verbal instructions must guide their partners around all the obstacles of chairs and moving people from one chair to the other. No physical contact of any kind is allowed.

4. Reverse roles and play again.

Variations

1. Reduce the instructions to one word at a time.

57.   INTRODUCTIONS

Another ice-breaker, this may seem to be less of a game and simply a way of letting everyone else know who they are. The fun comes into its own when a number of additional elements of information are introduced, especially if they are blatantly fictional.

Equipment

•   A chair for each Player.

Setting up

1.   Sit everyone in a circle.
2.   Choose a Starter.
3.   Indicate the direction of play.

Playing

1.   The Starter stands up and says **My name is** . . . . . and adds his/her first name.
     + *EXAMPLE: My name is Nicholas.*

2.   The next Player stands up and says **My name is** . . . . **and that is** . . . . putting in their own first name and then naming and pointing out the appropriate previous Player.
     + *EXAMPLE: My name is Louise and that is Nicholas.*

3.   The third Player stands up and says **My name is** . . . . . **and that is** . . . **and that is** . . . . . putting in their own first name and then naming and pointing out the two appropriate previous Players.
     + *EXAMPLE: My name is Sally and that is Louise and that is Nicholas.*

4.   This continues around the circle until everyone has had a go.

57. INTRODUCTIONS

If the group is new or recently formed get the Players to stick with their real names.

Variations

1. Keep it going around the circle more than once. In the second round Players can add their family name. In the third round they can add their age and so on.

2. If the group is well established the game can be played equally well with fictitious names and information.

3. The game can also be played using various categories of names with the Players adopting the names of historical characters or well known personalities.

58. I SPY

This is a game that must be known, in some form or another, across the entire planet and which has probably been played for centuries if not millennia. Familiarity should not lead to contempt. Its wide appeal is due to the fact that it is a good game, one that can be played anywhere and at any time as long as there are at least two people prepared to play.

Equipment

* A chair for each Player.

Setting up

1. Sit everyone in a circle.
2. Choose a Volunteer.

Playing

1. The Volunteer chooses an object in the room without disclosing what it is.

2. Once the Volunteer has chosen an object he/she then says the following **I spy with my little eye something beginning with** . . . . . adding the first letter of the name of their chosen object.

3. The other Players must try and guess what the object is.

4. If a Player guesses correctly it is then his/her turn to choose an object and say **I spy with my little eye something beginning with** . . . . to start the game again.

5. If everyone gives up without guessing, the object must be revealed and the Volunteer chooses another object.

Variations

1.   Limit Players to the number of guesses they may make.

2.   Use a predetermined location other than the room from which to choose
     objects.

     +   *EXAMPLE: A zoo, a hospital, a railway station, a museum, a
         department store, a supermarket, a farm and so on.*

ZOO LIST

Lion

Mane

Penguin

Python

Scales

Iguana

Peacock

Parrot

Feather

Orang-utang

Alligator

Tail

Camel

Hump

Giraffe

Hyena

Emu

Beak

Claw

Keeper

Leopard

Spots

Cage

Vivarium

59. JAIL BREAK

Another chair swapping game with more opportunity for mayhem than most others.

Equipment

- A chair for each Player.

Setting up

1. Put Players into Pairs.
2. Number each Pair from 1 to however many Pairs there are.
3. Choose one Volunteer Pair.
4. All the Pairs place their chairs about the room at random. These chairs do not have to be placed in any particular position relating to the Pairs but the Players must be able to hold hands when they are sitting paired up.
5. The Volunteer Pair place their chairs in the middle of the room - these must be positioned back to back. This is the jail.

Playing

1. One of the Volunteers in jail calls out any three of the numbers allocated to the Pairs. The Volunteer may not call out his/her own number.

2. The three Pairs whose numbers have been called out must all change chairs. At the same time the Volunteer Pair in jail are allowed to try and get to a vacated pair of chairs.

3. The Volunteer in jail has the option to call out **Jail Break** instead of calling out three numbers. If this happens everybody must get up and find a new pair of chairs. Again the Volunteer Pair in jail try to get to a vacant pair of chairs.

4. Whichever Pair is left standing when all the chairs are taken must go to the jail in the centre and sit on the chairs whereupon the game begins again.

5. Pairs must remain linked at all times by holding hands. The Players may sit in any two chairs as long as they can continue to hold hands.

6. In the event that a Pair of Players cannot occupy two chairs and remain linked because of rearrangements elsewhere they must both go to jail.

60. KALEIDOSCOPE

Memory can be notoriously fickle and the opportunity to practice the retention of facts in a fun way can be extremely useful.

Equipment

- A chair for each Player.

Setting up

1. Choose six Volunteers and stand them in a line.
2. Get everyone else to sit in a semi-circle facing the Volunteers.

Playing

1. Name each of the Volunteers a different colour.
   + *EXAMPLE: Red, Blue, Green, Yellow, White, Orange.*
     Violet, Scarlet, Indigo, Vermillion, Veridian, Crimson.

2. Get the seated Players to close and cover their eyes.

3. Rearrange the Volunteers.

4. Tell the seated Players to open their eyes and name the Volunteers by their correct colour.

   This game is best played quickly without giving those seated the chance to memorise who is which colour.

Variations

1. The Volunteers can be tagged with numbers, names of famous people, names of animals, and so on - the categories are endless.

61. KILLER

If you want the opposite of mayhem but with all the intensity of a more active game, this is the one to choose. Played in complete silence and seated in chairs it produces levels of concentration and paranoia unmatched by many other games.

Equipment

- A chair for each Player.

Setting up

1. Sit everyone in a circle.
2. Get everyone to close their eyes.
3. Impose a strict rule of silence. There is only one exception to this rule which is when you call out the name of an Accuser.
4. Walk around the outside of the circle and choose a number of people - about one in ten or fifteen is a good balance. Indicate your choice by tapping that Player on the shoulder. They are Killers.

Playing

1. On your command everyone opens their eyes and the game begins.

2. The Killers kill other Players by winking at them.

3. Any Player who is winked at counts silently to three and then puts his/her hands on their head to indicate that he/she is dead. Once dead Players are out of the game and cannot communicate with anyone.

4. A Killer cannot kill another Killer. Make this very clear otherwise you will get cries of, 'It's not fair, I just winked at him and he didn't die!'

5. While the Killers are at work everyone else must be on the lookout. If someone suspects another Player of being a killer the he/she must put up their hand. The Player wishing to make an accusation cannot be killed whilst his/her hand is up. When you call their name the Accuser must make their accusation.

6. If the Player making the accusation is correct the Killer is dead and must place his/her hands on his/her head.

7. If the accusation is wrong the Player who made the accusation is dead and must put his/her hands on his/her head.

8. The game ends when all the Killers are identified or when all other Players are dead and one or more Killers are left.

Variations

1. Remove the immunity from an Accuser so that he/she can still be killed whilst his/her hand is up.

2. Leave out the rule that says a Killer may not kill another Killer.

3. Introduce a rule preventing a Killer from accusing someone else of being a Killer.

4. Be mean. Make everyone a Killer or choose no one at all and see how long it is before the group realises what you have done.

The potential for confusion in this game is enormous. Information can bombard players from both directions and can easily cause an overload. Practice makes it easier to cope, but then you can always increase the complexity.

Equipment

- A chair for each Player.
- Two small objects of similar shape and size but of different appearance. These are the Knick and the Knack.

  + *EXAMPLE: A white tennis ball and a yellow tennis ball.*

Setting up

1. Sit everyone in a circle.
2. Choose a Starter.
3. Give the Knick and the Knack to the Starter.

Playing

1. The Starter passes the Knick to the Player on their right and states **This is a Knick.** Player 1 says **A what?** The Starter answers **A Knick.**

2. Player 1 passes the object on to Player 2 and states **This is a Knick.** Player 2 asks Player 1 **A what?** and Player 1 asks the Starter **A what?** The Starter replies to Player 1 **A Knick.** who replies in turn to Player 2 **A Knick.**

3. The object is passed in this way right around the circle. Each time it is passed on to the next Player the question **A what?** must pass all the way back to the Starter and the answer **A Knick.** must pass all the way back again before the object is passed on to the next Player with the statement **This is a Knick.**

4.   At the same time that the Knick is being passed around the circle in one direction the Knack is being passed in the other.   All the same rules apply just the name and direction of play is different.

Equipment for variation 1

* Additional pairs of small objects of similar shape and size but of different appearance.
    + *EXAMPLE: A red pepper and a green pepper, an envelope and a folded sheet of paper.*

Variations

1.   Once the Knick and the Knack are on the move start more objects going in both directions with the same rules applying to the additional Knick-Knacks.

2.   Be literal and call the objects what they are instead of a Knick and a Knack.

63. LAUGHING GAME

A very simple game that rarely lasts for very long.

Equipment

- A chair for each Player.

Setting up

1. Sit everyone in a circle.

2. Choose a Starter.

3. Indicate the direction of play.

Playing

1. The Starter says **Ha.**

2. The next Player says **Ha, ha.**

3. The next Player says **Ha, ha, ha.**

4. This continues around the circle indefinitely with each Player saying an additional **Ha.**

5. Anyone who laughs or messes up the number of times he/she says **Ha** is out and the game begins again with the next Player.

64.   LETTER BAN

The best results from this game are to be had from older players who have the language skills to cope with it. That is no reason not to introduce it to younger players, however, as the sooner they come to grips with the complexities of language the better. This game can be played with large and small groups or in pairs with equal success.

Equipment

- A chair for each Player.
- Alphabet Cards.

Setting up

1. Sit everyone in a circle.
2. Choose a card at random or use preselected cards and questions.

Playing

1. Ask each Player in turn a question.

2. The Players must answer as sensibly as they can with one proviso: - they must not use any words containing the letter you chose.
   + *EXAMPLE: If the letter chosen is F the session may go something like this: -*
      Q: What do you call a reddish doglike creature that eats chickens?
      A   Player 1: Reynard.
      Q: How many Beatles were there?
      A   Player 2: One more than three.
      Q: What sort of creature is Kermit?
      A   Player 3: An amphibian hand-puppet.

3. Anyone who cannot answer or answers using the banned letter or hesitates and generally makes a mess of things is out.

65.   LETTER ROUND

A straightforward exercise of vocabulary that becomes increasingly difficult as it is played.

Equipment

- A chair for each Player.

Setting up

1. Sit everyone in a circle.
2. Choose a Starter.
3. Indicate the direction of play.

Playing

1. The Starter says a word beginning with the letter A.

2. Each Player in turn must also say a word beginning with the letter A.

3. This continues round and round the circle until someone cannot think of a word or repeats a word or generally makes a mess of things. This Player is then out.

4. The game then starts again with the next Player and the next letter of the alphabet.

Equipment for variation 2

- Alphabet Cards

Variations

1. Introduce a time limit for each Player to think of a word.

2.   Instead of successive letters of the alphabet use the Alphabet Cards to choose letters at random.

3.   Only allow specific types of word beginning with the letter.

   + *EXAMPLE: Nouns, verbs, adverbs, names of countries, and so on.*

4.   Instead of a word beginning with the chosen letter try playing with words that contain that letter. In addition to the basic rules of play anyone who says a word beginning with the chosen is also out.

   + *EXAMPLE: If the letter is A the word could be scratch.*

   *If the next Player says **armour** this Player is out.*

5.   Try playing the game with words that must contain the chosen letter more than once.

   + *EXAMPLE: If the letter is A the word could be **aa**rdvark.*

6.   Try playing the game fast with words that must not contain the chosen letter.

   + *EXAMPLE: If the banned letter is A the word could be fish.*

7.   Instead of a word beginning with the current letter try using prefix words

   + *EXAMPLE: If the prefix word is **dog** the round might go something like this: **dog**fish, **dog**wood, **dog**-collar, and so on.*

66. LONG DISTANCE

Another form of trust exercise in which players have to listen carefully for the instructions intended for them, trusting that they will make their journey safely. All these games in which players are deprived of one or more of their senses make useful introductions to work on understanding what we are pleased to call 'disability'.

Equipment

- A chair for each Player.

Setting up

1. Put everyone into Pairs.
2. The Players name themelves A and B.
3. The A Players go to one end of the room and close their eyes. They must then keep their eyes closed throughout the game.
4. The B Players scatter the A Players chairs about the room to act as obstacles.
5. The B Players take their own chairs and stand behind them at the opposite end of the room.

Playing

1. Each B Player calls out instructions to their own partner and guides the partner to their seat in front at the opposite end of the room avoiding all the obstacles.

2. Reverse roles and play again.

Variations

1. Introduce a rule that any A Player to touch an obstacle or another A Player must stay put and is out of the game.

A game of observation that sounds as if it would last about twenty seconds but it is surprising how hard it can be to spot objects, especially when there is pressure on to find them.

Equipment

* A chair for each Player.
* A suitable object for hiding such as a pencil sharpener.

Setting up

1. Before the group enters the room place an object in an inconspicuous place so that it can be found without the need for anything to be moved.
2. When the group enters explain what you have done and tell the Players that nothing is to be moved or touched.
3. Impose a strict rule of silence.

Playing

1. On your command the Players move about the room searching for the object.

2. When a Player finds the object he/she makes no sign that he/she has done so but pretends to continue searching whilst counting silently to ten.

3. After counting silently to ten the Player sits down.

4. The last Player to find the object has the privilege of choosing and hiding the object for the next game.

Variations

1. Instead of simply naming the object to be found be a little more inventive and obscure in your description.

   + *EXAMPLE:* *If the object is a pencil sharpener describe it as* **a device used for sharpening everyday sticklike objects used for jotting things down by rotating these one at a time against a blade.**

2. Any number of objects can be hidden about your person. As you are mobile and in any case it is an unlikely place to look this can make the game all the more difficult.

   + *EXAMPLE:* *Pens, pencils and handkerchiefs are the most obvious items that are hard to spot.*

68. MAGNIFICENT DIDO

When I first heard of this game I did not understand it. The same was true when I first played it for, if it is played faithfully (as it was during my introduction), nothing happens. Every player sat in the correct position for about half an hour and that was it. It was one of the most puzzling, if relaxing, times I have spent. Subsequent experiences of the game have taught me that it can become one the most complex of situational improvisations based on a single premiss.

Equipment

- A chair for each Player including yourself.
- A block or dais on which to place your chair. This is not essential but adds to the atmosphere.
- An object to represent the Magnificent Dido (pronounced 'die-doh'). A bunch of keys will do but if you have an unusual and distinctive object that actually looks like - or is?!? - a Magnificent Dido then all the better.

Setting up

1. Sit everyone in a circle including yourself. Make sure your chair is slightly isolated or is on the block or dais. You are the King/Queen and everyone else is a member of your court.
2. Everyone in the circle except yourself must abide by the Majestic Laws and sit in a particular manner. That is - all the Players must sit with their right leg crossed over their left leg at the ankle and with their left arm folded over their right arm.
3. Once everyone is in position you then number the Players from 1 to however many there are. For the duration of the game each Player is to be referred to by their number and in no other way unless an official title is conferred upon a Player by you.
4. Impose a strict rule of silence.

Playing

As this is a game of situational improvisation the more elaborate the rituals the more fun the game. Also, the King/Queen greatly enjoys the position of supreme power and all flattery and subservience on the part of the Players will be greeted favourably.

1. Abiding by the Majestic Laws - sitting as described in complete silence and stillness is the prime objective of the game.

2. If anyone infringes the Majestic Laws then someone else is at liberty to make a complaint to the King/Queen. However, no one is allowed to speak without holding the Magnficent Dido - an artefact that is to be treated with the utmost reverence. Players must indicate their desire to speak by holding up their left hand and waiting.

3. If the King/Queen sees fit he/she will summon the Player and allow the Player to hold the Magnificent Dido. This Player is then at liberty to make a complaint.

4. Once a complaint has been made the Accused is summoned and given the chance to speak in his/her own defence. This can be built into an elaborate trial with a judge and jury, witnesses, and so on.

5. If the Accused is found guilty then he/she must pay a forfeit. Forfeits must range in degree of difficulty to fit the seriousness of the crime.

6. If the Accused is found to be innocent then the Accuser must pay a forfeit. Paying the forfeit wipes the slate clean.

7. A Player has the right to refuse a forfeit and is given three chances each forfeit increasing in severity. Any Player who refuses all three forfeits is taken away and executed - that is, he/she is out of the game.

Variations

1.   **Once** the game is established other important roles can be given to **Players**. The most important of these is the Keeper of the Magnificent Dido who has the responsibility of guarding the magnificent object and seeing that it is not maltreated when being handled by other Players. Then there is the Keeper of the Majestic Law who acts as judge in disputes and advises the King/Queen on points of Majestic Law. There is also the Chief Snide who acts as a spy - watching for Players who might be breaking Majestic Law. The more jobs the merrier. If everyone has one then you can get twisted into some interesting situations, especially when there is the possibility of promotion from, or demotion to, such posts as Second Assistant to the Apprentice Bootlicker.

2.   Instead of a forfeit wiping the slate clean misdemeanours accumulate. Then three convictions lead to execution.

Dido *n. U.S. colloqual. [19* th *Century origin unknown.]*   An antic, a mischievous trick, a caper, a prank

69. MATCHBOX, TIN, JAM-JAR, BUCKET

A restrictive form of word association game that can, nonetheless, lead to some extremely creative responses and heated argument about whether or not a given word is acceptable.

Equipment

- A chair for each Player.

Setting up

1. Sit everyone in a circle.
2. Choose a Starter.
3. Indicate the direction of play.

Playing

1. The Starter says one of the following words **Matchbox, Tin, Jam-Jar, Bucket.**

2. The next Player must immediately say a word that is connected with the one just called and then add one of the four words without a pause. This continues round the circle.

3. Anyone who repeats a response, hesitates, fumbles, forgets, makes a dubious connection or generally makes a mess of things is out and the game starts again with the next Player.

   + *EXAMPLE: A game may go somthing like this: The Starter:* **Jam-Jar.** *Player 1:* **Marmalade - Matchbox.** *Player 2:* **Beetle - Tin.** *Player 3:* **Paint - Bucket.** *Player 4:* **Water - Jam-Jar** ......

Variations

1. Change the four key words.

It takes a little while for some players to get the hang of this especially the 'greeting' element. However, it is well worth persisting as it extremely enjoyable.

Equipment

- None.

Setting up

1. Make sure the room is clear of all obstacles.
2. Tell the members of the group to spread out and close their eyes. Players must keep their eyes closed throughout.
3. Impose a strict rule of silence.
4. Move amongst the Players and choose a Murderer or Murderers. Indicate your choice by tapping the Player or Players on the shoulder. The number of Murderers depends on the size of the group but one for every ten to fifteen Players is a good ratio.

Playing

1. On your command everyone begins to move slowly and carefully about the room with their arms stretched out in front of them.

2. When contact is made between two Players they stand face to face and greet each other in the following way:

    (a) One Player puts his/her hands palm up.

    (b) The other Player puts his/her hands palm down.

    (c) The palms down Player claps the palm up Player's hands three times.

    (d) Hands are then reversed and the above is repeated.

3. A Murderer, however, has the option to move away after the first half of the greeting thereby killing the other Player.

4. When a victim realises that the second half of the greeting is not forthcoming and that he/she is dead the Player then opens his/her eyes and makes his/her way to the side of the room.

5. A Murderer cannot be killed.

6. The game ends when everyone has been murdered and only the Murderer or Murderers remain in the playing area.

Variations

1. Include one or more Detectives - choosing them at the same time that you choose the Murders. Indicate your choice by tapping a Player or Players on the head. The inclusion of Detectives changes the rules slightly.

    (1.) When a victim realises that he/she is dead the Player must scream or say **I'm dead**. This gives the Detectives some idea of where the Murderer is in the room.

    (2.) When a Detective meets someone and gets no response to the first half of the greeting the Detective, keeping eyes closed, may make a grab for the Murderer. If the Detective manages to catch hold of a Murderer that Murderer is out.

    (3.) Detectives cannot be killed so this game ends when there are only Detectives left in the playing area.

2. Be mean and choose no Murderers.

71. MUSICAL TOUCHINGS

An observation game that requires a deal of concentration in respect of the posture of other players. A useful exercise in relation to movement and characterization.

Equipment

- A source of music.

Setting up

1. Put everyone into Pairs.
2. The Players name themselves A and B.
3. A's stand in a circle facing outwards. B's stand facing their partners.

Playing

1. All the B Players make contact with their A partners by touching any part of the partner's body with a hand.

2. A Players make that part of their body prominent without being too obvious.

3. Start the music. All the B Players must walk around the outside of the circle.

4. When the music stops each B Player must make contact with whichever A happens to be standing opposite by touching the correct part of the A Player's body - the part touched by their partner.

5. Any B Player who makes contact with the wrong part of the body is out along with the A Player who was touched in the wrong place.

6. The music starts again and the game continues in this manner until one Pair is left.

72.   MY GRANDPA'S CUPBOARD

Memory, concentration, and association are useful skills in this quiet game. It helps if Grandpa keeps unusual things in his cupboard.

Equipment

- A chair for each Player.

Setting up

1. Sit everyone in a circle.
2. Choose a Starter.
3. Indicate the direction of play.

Playing

1. The Starter begins the game by saying **My Grandpa keeps . . . . . in his cupboard.** Naming an object beginning with the letter A.
   + *EXAMPLE: My Grandpa keeps an **aardvark** in his cupboard.*

2. The next Player must then say **My Grandpa keeps an aardvark and a . . . . . in his cupboard.** Naming an object beginning with the letter B.
   + *EXAMPLE: My Grandpa keeps an aardvark and a **battleship** in his cupboard.*

3. The next Player repeats the sentence and names the previous two objects and adds one beginning with C.
   + *EXAMPLE: My Grandpa keeps an aardvark, a battleship and a **chrysanthemum** in his cupboard.*

4. This continues round and round the circle for as long as the group can manage. Once the alphabet has been gone through once go back to A and continue through again.

5. Anyone who misses an object or repeats something in a second or later round is out. The game starts again with the next Player.

Variations

1. Restrict the list of objects to things that would actually fit in a cupboard. It is wise to indicate what size the cupboard is before you start.

2. Restrict the list of objects to kitchen cupboard items.

LIST OF OBJECTS

An apple

A brick

A duck

An egg

Fish

A gun

A hammer

Ink

Jam

A mango

Nails

Oranges

A pineapple

A quince

Raddishes

Sugar

A tin

An umberella

A vase

A wasp

A xylophone

A yam

A zip

73. NAMES IN A CIRCLE

Experience suggests that this game works better when played quickly. New players will, however, be hesitant - trying to work out whose name it is safe to call. Hence Variation 2.

Equipment

- One chair less than the number of Players in the group.
- Chalk.

Setting up

1. Choose a Volunteer.
2. Sit everyone in a circle with the Volunteer standing in the middle.
3. Chalk a circle on the floor around the Volunteer.

Playing

1. The Volunteer says his/her own name and then the name of a Player sitting in the circle.

2. The Volunteer and Player then swap places.

3. The Player who is now in the middle must be standing inside the chalk circle before saying his/her own name and then the name of a Player sitting in the circle.

4. These two Players then swap places.

5. This continues with the following taken into account - a Player can only stand in the middle three times. If the name of any Player sitting in the circle is called for a fourth time (that is, the Player has already stood in the centre three times) the Player replies by saying **No.**

6. If the Player in the middle is told **No** then the Player in the middle is out.

7. The game starts again with a new Volunteer.

Variations

1. Change the number of times any Player is allowed to stand in the middle.

2. Impose a time limit on the Player in the middle choosing and naming a Player.

Another introductory game that works just as well with players who know each other well. Although only four variations are given, this game has the potential for many more.

Equipment

- A chair for each Player.
- A tennis ball.

Setting up

1. Sit everyone in a circle.
2. Choose a Starter and give the Starter the tennis ball.
3. Indicate the initial direction of play.

Playing

1. The Starter says his/her own name clearly and then passes the tennis ball to the next Player.

2. The next Player says his/her own name and then passes on the tennis ball.

3. This continues right around the circle until the tennis ball is back with the Starter.

4. The Starter then throws the ball to any other Player who must then say the name of the Player who threw the ball.

5. This Player then throws the ball to another Player who must then say the name of the Player who threw the ball.

6. The game continues continues in this fashion until everyone knows everyone else's name.

Variations

1. When first names are known add surnames and play again.

2. If Players know each other well invent new and unusual names. Anyone making a mistake is out.

3. Play using the names of historical or fictional characters.

4. Instead of saying the name of the Player who threw the ball each Player must say the name of the Player he/she is about to throw the ball to.

LIST OF FICTIONAL CHARACTERS
Cinderella
Humpty Dumpty
Toad of Toad Hall
Willy Wonka
Oliver Twist
Long John Silver
James Bond
Sherlock Holmes
Aladdin
Homer Simpson
Marge Simpson
Superman
The Scarlet Pimpernel
Miss Marple
Hercule Poirot
Little Bo Peep
Little Jack Horner
Robin Hood

Sifting information from a background of distraction can be extremely difficult yet it is an increasingly important skill in these days of information overload. A little practice is not only useful but can lead to some extremely interesting results when players get their wires crossed when listening to several readings at once.

Equipment

- A large selection of newspaper cuttings.
- A chair for each Player.

Setting up

1. Split the group into threes.
2. The Players name themelves A, B and C.

Playing

1. A reads a newspaper story to B.

2. Whilst A is reading C attempts to distract B. C can do anything except touch either A or B or drown out A's voice with noise.

3. When A has finished reading B is tested on how much information he/she took in.

4. Rotate the Players so that everyone has a turn at playing each role.

Variations

1. The distraction offered can be a second newspaper story being read out.

There is pressure on both sides in this game. Not only must the volunteer work out the place or person involved, but those questioned must also be able to answer appropriately. And as the sample questions and answers show, there is a great deal of ambiguity involved.

Equipment

• A chair for each Player.

Setting up

1. Sit everyone in a circle.
2. Choose a Volunteer.

Playing

1. The Volunteer leaves the room.

2. The other Players decide on the name of a person or place that the Volunteer must identify.

3. The Volunteer returns and questions each Player in turn in an attempt to find out who or what has been chosen.

4. All questions must be worded so that they elicit a **Yes** or **No** answer.

5. If the answer to a question is **Yes** that is the answer that is given and the questioning moves on to the next Player .

6. If the answer to a question is **No** the Player must give a little more information. This is done by saying **No, it's not** . . . . . adding a name that is relevant to the question and which also begins with the same letter as the name of the person or place that the Volunteer is trying to discover.

+ *EXAMPLE: If the original name chosen is* **Berlin** *questioning may go something like this: -*

Q Volunteer: Is it a country?

A Player 1: No, it's not **B***olivia.*

Q Volunteer: Is it a man?

A Player 2: No, it's not the Venerable **B***ede.*

Q Volunteer: Is it a fictional character?

A Player 3: No, it's not Tom **B***ombadil.*

Q Volunteer: Is it a city?

A Player 4: Yes.

Q Volunteer: Is it a city in England?

A Player 5: No, it's not **B***irmingham.*

Q Volunteer: Is it a European city?

A Player 6: Yes.

Q Volunteer: Is it **Berlin***?*

A Player 6: Yes.

The Volunteer has guessed correctly and Player 6 now leaves the room and the game continues.

7. If a Player cannot answer a **No** question with correct information that Player is out.

8. Play continues until the Volunteer discovers what was decided upon by the other Players or until there are no Players left to question.

Variations

1. Limit the game to a set number of questions.

If I had to choose a favourite, this would be it. I could not really say why as it is no more or less exotic or exciting than any other game in this book. Perhaps it is because it is one of the first I played with a group. Be that as it may, it requires a great degree of concentration, especially as the numbers are fixed to the chairs rather than the players. It also has a goal as well as allowing players to stay in the game, no matter how many times they make an error.

Equipment

- A chair for each Player.

Setting up

1. Sit everyone in a circle with a single chair-sized gap.
2. Starting on one side of the gap number the chairs from 1 to however many chairs there are. Players adopt the number of the chair they are sitting on at any given time in the game. It is important to stress this to new Players.

Playing

The game is played to the same rhythm as *CLAP-TRAP* - a four beat cycle the whole cycle lasting about two seconds each beat of equal duration.

1. The aim of the game is to sit in Chair No 1.

2. Once the rhythm is established the Player on Chair No1 starts. As with *CLAP-TRAP* everything happens on the two finger-click beats. On the first of these beats the Player says the number of the chair he/she is sitting on and on the second of these beats the Player says any other number providing this number is not greater than the number of chairs in the game.

3. On the next cycle of finger-click beats the Player whose chair number was called out second must repeat the number of the chair he/she is sitting on and must then say any other chair number.

4. This continues until someone misses a beat, muddles numbers, says a number that does not exist or generally messes things up.

5. The offending Player must leave the chair and take up residence in the chair with the highest number. Everyone else who was above that player moves down one chair to fill up the gap adopting the number of the chair they have just moved to.

+ *EXAMPLE: If 25 people are playing and the Player on Chair 7 makes a mistake - that Player must go to Chair 25. Players on Chairs 8 to 25 all move down one chair to occupy Chairs 7 to 24. Players sitting on Chairs 6 to 1 stay where they are.*

6. Once Players have moved seats the Player on Chair 1 restarts the game.

Variations

1. If there are twenty-six Players or less in the group tag the chairs with successive letters of the alphabet.

78. OCCUPATIONS

A very simple exercise which can be challenging as players have the double task of miming accurately and clearly whilst at the same time trying to produce a mime that will confuse other players.

Equipment

- A chair for each Player.

Setting up

1. Sit everyone in a circle.
2. Choose a Starter.
3. Indicate the direction of play.

Playing

1. Everyone thinks of a job or activity.

2. Each Player in turn stands in the centre of the circle and mimes an activity.

3. When Players think they know what is being mimed they call out with guesses. The next player takes a turn when the activity has been guessed correctly.

Variations

1. Award points for correct guesses.

2. Play it as a team game.

79.   ONE TO TEN

Although it is easy to learn, this game becomes increasingly difficult to play as there are a limited number of letters with which numbers begin.

Equipment

*   A chair for each Player.

Setting up

1.   Sit everyone in a circle.
2.   Choose a Starter.
3.   Indicate the direction of play.

Playing

1.   The Starter says the number **One** and adds the name of an object beginning with the letter O.
     + *EXAMPLE:* ***One** onion.*

2.   This is then repeated quickly round the circle by each Player in turn and finally repeated by the Starter again.

3.   Player 1 then says **One onion and two** . . . . . adding something beginning with the letter T.
     + *EXAMPLE:* ***One onion and two** tigers.*

4.   This is repeated quickly round the circle by each Player in turn and finally repeated by Player 1 again. Player 2 then adds to the formula.
     + *EXAMPLE:* ***One** onion and **two** tigers and **three** trombones.*

5.   This continues around the circle with each Player adding the next number and naming an object that starts with the same letter as the number.

+ *EXAMPLE: One onion and two tigers and three trombones and four fish.*

6. The game continues in this manner.

   + *EXAMPLE: One onion and two tigers and three trombones and four fish and five frogs and six shoes and seven sharks and eight elephants and nine natterjacks and ten tents.*

7. Any Player who repeats an object, forgets to include something or generally makes a mess of things is out.

8. The game starts again with the next Player.

80.   ON THE SURFACE

A more advanced exercise in concentration that involves the use of a limited set of senses. If nothing else, it will demonstrate the degree to which we depend on our eyes.

Equipment

* A chair for each Player.

Setting up

1. Put everyone into pairs.
2. The Players name themselves A and B.
3. Pairs take their chairs to various parts of the room and sit facing each other.

Playing

1. All the A Players close their eyes.

2. The B Players take their A partners and stand them up and then turn them around three or four times to confuse their sense of direction.

3. The B Players then lead their partners to four or five different locations in the room confusing directions on the way.

4. At each location a B Player puts one of the A partner's hands on a different type of surface and A feels the surface.

5. The B Players then return all the A's to their seats where they sit and open their eyes.

6. All the A Players must try to identify the surfaces they have touched and then reveal the guesses to their partners.

7.   Reverse the roles and play again.

Variations

1.   Instead of just identifying what they have touched the A Players must also try and recreate the route they took to get to the objects and surfaces that they felt.

81.   ON THE TABLE

A game that can be played almost anywhere and at any time - provided your pockets are well stocked with all manner of exotic objects.

Equipment

- A chair for each Player.
- A table.
- An assortment of twenty or so smallish objects initially kept in a number of your pockets.

Setting up

1. Sit everyone in a semicircle with the table in the centre where everyone can see the surface.
2. Stand behind the table and tell everyone to watch carefully.

Playing

1. Take the objects from your pockets one by one and place them on the table.

2. Once all the objects are on display give the Players fifteen seconds to look.

3. Tell everyone to close their eyes. Remove an object from the table and conceal it in the pocket from which you took it.

4. Then tell everyone to open their eyes. The Players must identify the object that has been removed on opening their eyes.

5. Continue in this way removing and replacing various objects and combinations of objects and changing their position on the table.

Variations

1. When you have finished Players must say which pockets the objects
    were taken from and in which order.

LIST OF OBJECTS

A used postage stamp on an envelope corner

An unused postage stamp

A thimble

A coin

A ring

A nail file

A pencil

A crayon

A pen

A paintbrush

A ticket

A wrapped sweet

A paper clip

A rubber

A button

A safety pin

A feather

A rubber band

A match

A drawing pin

An earring

A key

A teaspoon

A paper clip

A marble

A pebble

82. OPPOSITES

Quick thinking is needed in this game to avoid making a mistake. It also takes an effort on the part of players to avoid giving correct information.

Equipment

* A chair for each player.

Setting up

1. Choose a Volunteer.
2. Sit everyone in a circle with the Volunteer in the midddle.
3. Choose a Starter.
4. Indicate the direction of play.

Playing

1. Beginning with the Starter each Player asks the Volunteer one question which can only be answered **Yes** or **No**.

2. The Volunteer must answer immediately with the opposite of what is true.

3. This continues round and round the circle until the Volunteer answers incorrectly within the context of the game.

4. The Player who asked the question that the Volunteer answered incorrectly then takes a turn in the middle and the game starts again.
    + *EXAMPLE: The Volunteer is John from London and he is sixteen years old.*

    > *Q: Are you John?*
    > *A: No.*
    > *Q: Do you come from London?*
    > *A: No.*

Q: Are you eighteen?

A: **No.**

Which is the incorrect response in the context of the game.

The Player in the middle is Louise she has auburn hair and is wearing black shoes.

Q: Is your name Louise?

A: No.

Q: Are you wearing black shoes?

A: No.

Q: Is your hair auburn?

A: **Yes.**

Which is the incorrect response in the context of the game.

83. OVER THE WALL

It is to this game more than any other that the strictures on safety and responsibility outlined in the notes refer. That said, this makes an excellent situation game in which the players can develop a story and characters. You can, therefore, give the group a specific situation to work from before the game begins or use the game as a starting point. After all, most escape stories tell of what was escaped from, not what happened to the escapees once they were free.

Equipment

- A room with blackout.
- A large quantity of chairs, tables, boxes, and the like.
- A light - such as a powerful torch or spotlight capable of throwing a tightly focused beam.

Setting up

1. Using all the chairs, tables and boxes build a barrier from wall to wall across the room.
2. Put all the members of the group at one end of the room and stand at the other with the light.

Playing

1. Turn out all the lights.

2. Players must make their way from one end of the room to the other crossing the barrier. Once a Player reaches your end he/she is safe.

3. Anyone caught moving by the beam of light is out and must stay put. You can move about freely and turn the light on and off at will.

4. The game ends when all members of the group are safe or caught.

84. PACKING MY BAG

This is a game from my own youth. Despite all those intervening years, I still enjoy packing my bag.

Equipment

* A chair for each Player.

Setting up

1. Sit everyone in a circle.
2. Choose a Starter.
3. Indicate the direction of play.

Playing

1. The Starter begins the game by saying **I packed my bag and in my bag I put a . . . . .** adding any object that the Starter wishes to pack in the bag.
   + *EXAMPLE: I packed my bag and in my bag I put **a dog.***

2. The next Player then says **I packed my bag and in my bag I put a dog and a . . . . . .** adding an additional item of his/her own.
   + *EXAMPLE: I packed my bag and in my bag I put a dog and **a toothbrush.***

3. This continues round and round the circle with each Player repeating everything that has gone before and then adding an item.

4. The game goes on until someone forgets an item, gets the items in the wrong order, adds an item already included or generally messes things up. This Player is then out.

5. The game starts again with the next Player.

Variations

1. Instead of starting the game again every time a Player is out keep the list going - remembering to omit the item added by any Player who has since been eliminated.

2. Limit the list of items to things that would actually fit in a bag. You will have to specify the size and type of bag to avoid arguements.

3. Have a specific type of activity or situation in mind and pack the bag appropriately.
   + *EXAMPLE: A holiday bag, a school bag, and so on.*

HOLIDAY BAG LIST

Sunglasses

Suncream

Sun-hat

Flip-flops

Frisbee

Camera

Roll of film

Flippers

Snorkel

Swimwear

Towel

Beach-ball

Shorts

Tee shirt

Insect repellent

First aid kit

Passport

Phrase book

Tickets

Playing cards

No memory required here, just a keen eye if you are the Volunteer or a facial expression that would be the envy of any poker player if you are the one sitting in the circle holding the newspaper behind your back.

Equipment

- A chair for each Player.
- A rolled up newspaper, taped to keep it in a roll.

Setting up

1. Choose a Volunteer.
2. Sit everyone in a circle with the Volunteer in the midddle.

Playing

1   The Volunteer closes his/her eyes.

2. Give the newspaper to any Player. It is then passed around the circle from Player to Player behind their backs.

3. When the newspaper is in motion tell the Volunteer to open his/her eyes. The Volunteer must now try to establish the position of the newspaper.

4. If the Volunteer believes that someone is concealing the newspaper behind their back the Volunteer points to the Player.

5. The Volunteer continues to challenge Players in this way until he/she makes a correct challenge. Then the Volunteer and Player caught with the newspaper change places and the game begins again.

Another exercise in vocabulary, this time making use of adjectives and leading to descriptions of a cat that stretch the imagination.

Equipment

- A chair for each Player.
- A set of Alphabet Cards.

Setting up

1. Sit everyone in a circle.
2. Choose a Starter.
3. Indicate the direction of play.

Playing

1. The Starter chooses an Alphabet Card at random. This is the key letter for the game.

2. Each Player in turn repeats the following: **The Parson's cat is a/an . . . cat.** inserting an adjective that begins with the key letter and which has not been used by any other Player.
   + *EXAMPLE: The Starter chose the letter **F**.*

   > *Player 1: The Parson's cat is a **fastidious** cat.*
   > *Player 2: The Parson's cat is a **fluffy** cat.*
   > *Player 3: The Parson's cat is a **furious** cat.*
   > *Player 4: The Parson's cat is a **fat** cat.*

3. Anyone who repeats, hesitates, invents an adjective, or generally makes a mess of things is out.

4. Play starts again with the next Player.

Clarity and care of movement are requisites for this game as well as the ability to see where an action has sufficient ambiguity that it might actually be something else.

Equipment

- A chair for each Player.

Setting up

1. Sit everyone in a circle.
2. Choose a Starter.
3. Indicate the direction of play.
4. Impose a strict rule of silence.

Playing

1. The Starter thinks of an object and then mimes this in use.
   + *EXAMPLE: Starter paints a wall with a paintbrush.*

2. Once the object has been mimed in use it is passed to Player 1 who mimes whatever he/she thinks has been given to him/her in use.
   + *EXAMPLE: Player 1 conducts an orchestra with a baton.*

1. The mimed object is passed around the circle in this fashion. When it reaches the end all the Players in turn tell the rest what they were miming.

Variations

1. Instead of each Player saying what was being mimed all the Players must try to guess what each Player was miming.

88.   PASS THE POST

A great deal of co-ordination and trust is required here, especially if the group progresses to moving players over their heads. The results are rewarding.

Equipment

- None.

Setting up

1.   Choose a Volunteer.

Playing

1.   The Volunteer lies on the floor flat on his/her back with eyes closed stiff as a post.

2.   Ten or twelve Players surround the Volunteer and pick him/her up and hold him/her in a horizontal position.

3.   The Volunteer is then passed to the hands of other Players.

4.   As Players become free of their burden they move themselves into a position where they can take the Volunteer again ensuring that the Volunteer is moving freely and continuously in a horizontal position.

5.   Everyone takes a turn at being passed around.

Variations

1.   Once members of the group trust each other and you are satisfied with their dexterity the Volunteers should be passed around over the heads of the other Players on extended arms.

89.   PICTURE IT

This game puts memory to the test by using the body as a means of expressing what is being recalled. More than most, this game points up the need to understand what is being recalled to make that recall accurate.

Equipment

- A chair for each Player.
- At least six pictures or photographs of groups of people.

Setting up

1.   Sit everyone in a circle.

Playing

1.   Pass the pictures around the circle. No one is allowed to look at any picture for more than ten seconds.

2.   Once all the Players have seen all the pictures split the group into several smaller groups.

3.   Number each group from one to however many groups there are.

4.   Group 1 must now to the best of its collective memory and ability reproduce the position of the people in the first picture. Group 2 does the same with the second picture, and so on.

Variations

1.   You can make this game as simple or as detailed as you like. Reproducing positions of people may be ranked as fairly easy. To make the game more difficult you can demand that facial expressions and body language must also match.

90.   POCKETFUL OF BAKED BEANS

Perhaps the prohibition on laughter is what ultimately inspires it in this game. On the other hand, the silliness of the thing may be the main reason. Whatever the cause, you are likely to find that this game will touch the funny bones, especially of young players, and end in helpless hysterics.

Equipment

* A chair for each Player.

Setting up

1. Choose a Starter.
2. Choose a Volunteer.
3. Sit everyone in a circle except the Volunteer who sits in the middle.
4. Indicate the direction of play.

Playing

1. The Starter asks the Volunteer a question - any question the Starter cares to choose.
   + *EXAMPLE: What is your favourite colour?*

2. The Volunteer must respond with the phrase **A pocketful of baked beans** without so much as the hint of a smile, let alone a giggle, a laugh or any other unseemly behaviour.

3. If the Volunteer keeps a straight face he/she stays in the centre and the next Player asks a question to which the Volunteer must respond again with the reply **A pocketful of baked beans.**

4. If the Volunteer smiles or laughs in response to a question he/she then changes places with the Player who asked the question that prompted the expression of mirth and the game starts again with the next Player asking a question.

Variations

1. Change the response to something else like **Sausages**, **In a matchbox**, **In your dreams**, or whatever takes your fancy. Questions can then be tailored by Players in an attempt to make the player in the middle laugh.

    + *EXAMPLE: If the response is* **In a matchbox.**

    > Q: Where would you find the Taj Mahal?
    >
    > A: **In a matchbox.**
    >
    > Q: What is the best way to travel from England to Australia?
    >
    > A: **In a matchbox.**
    >
    > Q: Where do you keep your matches?
    >
    > A: **In a matchbox.**

2. Make three or more responses available to the Volunteer who must swap between them without hesitation, a smile, a giggle or a laugh during rapid questioning by the other Players in turn.

    + *EXAMPLE: If the responses are **A pocketful of baked beans Sausages, In a matchbox, In your dreams.***

    > Q: *What is your name?*
    >
    > A: ***Sausages.***
    >
    > Q: *What is your favourite food?*
    >
    > A: ***In a matchbox.***
    >
    > Q: *How old are you?*
    >
    > A: ***In your dreams.***
    >
    > Q: *Do you have a favourite colour?*
    >
    > A: ***A pocketful of baked beans.***
    >
    > Q: *Where do you live?*
    >
    > A: ***In a matchbox.***
    >
    > Q: *Are you interested in sport?*
    >
    > A: ***In your dreams.***
    >
    > Q: *What is your most treasured possession?*
    >
    > A: ***A pocketful of baked beans.***

91. POINTS OF BALANCE

Although a simple exercise in movement and co-ordination this can still be great fun, especially when you make absurd demands.

Equipment

- None.

Setting up

1. Put Players into groups of three, four, five, or more.

Playing

1. Members of each group must produce a sculpture with their bodies using a predetermined number of points of balance.

   A point of balance is that part of the body that needs to make contact with the ground in order to keep the rest of the body balanced. Knees, elbows, buttocks, foreheads, fingers, can all be points of balance. A standing person uses two points of balance - their feet.

   Start simply by giving the group more points of balance than there are Players in the group.

2. Real skill comes into play when you then give the group less points of balance than there are Players as this means that at least one person must not make contact with the ground in any way.

92.   POINT TO POINT

This game requires a great deal of concentration which is surprising as it is something we tend to do without thinking when we walk along a busy pavement. However, as with many activities we do without thinking, the act of thinking about them causes problems.

Equipment

• None.

Setting up

1. Get every Player to stand in a place as far away from everyone else as possible.

Playing

1. Tell everyone to choose a spot on the floor some distance from themselves.

2. On your command all the Players must make for their own spot by moving in a straight line - walking without stopping and pacing themelves to avoid collision or contact with any of the other Players.

Variations

1. The method of travelling between the two points can be varied. Instead of walking Players might have to hop, walk backwards, walk sideways or take the fewest number of steps possible.

2. Every Player works with a partner with two legs held (or tied) together, Players in Pairs stand facing each other and the Player facing backwards is guided between the two points by the other Player.

93. PREDICAMENTS

Another game that requires a great deal of inventiveness with players having to be as honest to the demands of the game as they can without giving anything away.

Equipment

- A chair for each Player.

Setting up

1. Sit everyone in a circle.
2. Choose a Volunteer.

Playing

1. The Volunteer leaves the room.

2. The rest of the Players decide upon a predicament.
   + *EXAMPLE: Trapped in a lift, lost in the desert, and so on.*

3. The Volunteer returns to the room and tries to ascertain what the predicament is. This is done by asking one question of as many Players as necessary. The Volunteer asks **What would you do?**

4. Players are asked the question in turn and must answer as inventively as they can and to the point but giving away as little information as possible.
   + *EXAMPLE: If the predicament is trapped in a lift.*
     Player 1 A: I would sit down and wait.
     Player 2 A: I would shout loudly.

5. The Player who gives the predicament away is the next to go out of the room and the game begins again.

This game can be enormously frustrating for the volunteers as it is almost impossible to spot the squeezing by direct observation. Once they learn to look for signs elsewhere, especially in the facial expressions of players, then it becomes easier - but not much.

Equipment

* A chair for each Player

Setting up

1. Chose a Volunteer.
2. Sit everyone in a circle except the Volunteer who sits in the middle.

Playing

1. The Players in the circle all hold hands.

2. The Volunteer closes his/her eyes and counts slowly to twenty.

3. Whilst the Volunteer's eyes are closed you choose a Player in the circle by tapping that person on the shoulder.

4. The chosen Player must then sqeeze one of the neighbouring players hands that he/she is holding.

5. Each player passes on the squeeze - players may reverse direction if they wish but nobody is allowed to pause.

6. When the Volunteer has finished counting to twenty and opened his/her eyes he/she tries to locate the position of the squeeze.

7. If the Volunteer thinks that he/she can see the squeeze then he/she can challenge that Player.

8.   If the Volunteer makes a correct challenge and the Player is caught squeezing at that moment the Volunteer and Player swap places and the game begins again.

9.   If the Volunteer is wrong he/she stays in the midddle and the game continues.

95. QUESTIONS, QUESTIONS

Another old favourite that can be played almost anywhere and, with some ingenuity, can continue for some length of time.

Equipment

- A chair for each Player.

Setting up

1. Put the group into Pairs.
2. The Players name themselves A and B.

Playing

1. A asks B a question.

2. B must reply with a question.

3. A responds to B's question with a question.

4. This continues back and forth until either the A Player or B Player repeats a question, makes a statement, or just cannot think of anything to say.

5. The winner starts the next round.

> + *EXAMPLE:* A: *What's your name?*
> B: *Why do you ask?*
> A: *Why won't you tell me your name?*
> B: *Is it important that I do?*
> A: *What do you think?*
> B: *Why are you asking all these questions?*
> A: *Can't you give a straight answer?*

95.   QUESTIONS, QUESTIONS

Variations

1. Ban all stock questions which are used simply because Players cannot think of anything else.

    + *EXAMPLE:* What are all the bears doing in the woods today?

      What is the religious faith of the Pope?   (or any other religious leader.)

2. Play with tag teams of five or more Players in each team.   When someone is out the next team member moves up to replace that Player. The first team to exhaust all its Players loses.

3. Sit all the B's in a circle facing outwards.   Sit all the A's in a circle outside them facing inwards.   Choose an A Player to start.   A asks the B partner a question.   B responds with a question which he/she addresses to the A sitting clockwise of their partner.   This A Player then asks a question of his/her B Partner.   The game continues with questions zigzagging around the circle until someone is out.   The game then restarts with the next Player.

This was always a favourite with the groups I worked with and kept me on my toes as I was constantly having to think of new categories by which they could order themselves. It is as well to have a few new ones up your sleeve.

Equipment

- None.

Setting up

1. Impose a strict rule of silence.

Playing

1. On your command members of the group without speaking or writing things down must form a straight line in any particular order you give.

The easiest task for Players to perform is for you to ask them to line up in order of height. However, the categories you choose are bounded only by your imagination and the capabilities of the group - and any sadistic streak you may possess.

+ *EXAMPLE:*   *You might ask the group to line up in order of shoe size, age to the day, by house number, alphabetically by first or last name or alphabetically by the title or author of the book Players are reading at that time.*

97. REACH OUT

Although this game or exercise can be played for its own sake, for the fun of seeing what happens, it also makes a useful warm up for group work

Equipment

- A room with blackout and variable light control.

Setting up

1. Clear the room of all obstacles.
2. Everyone chooses a place to stand and the Players all close their eyes.

Playing

1. Reduce the level of light to the minimum necessary for you to see.

2. On your command everyone moves slowly around the room.

3. When one Player makes contact with another they both link hands leaving each with one hand free to link up with someone else.

4. Once each Player is linked to two other people (that is when both hands are taken up) he/she must stop moving.

5. No one must break into the chain that is forming but must find a free hand at the end.

6. When everyone is linked tell the Players to stay put and open their eyes. Bring up the lights so that they can see the chain that has been formed.

Variations

1. Impose a strict rule of silence.

98.   REARRANGEMENTS

This works best when the volunteer is unaware of what task you are going to ask to be performed. There are a number of games like this and they can be played in a mixed assortment - each round different from the last.

Equipment

*   A chair for each Player.

Setting up

1.   Sit everyone in a circle.
2.   Choose a Volunteer.
3.   Send the Volunteer out of the room.

Playing

1.   Once the Volunteer is out of the room some or all of the Players swap seats.

2.   The Volunteer is called back into the room and must rearrange the group the way it was before he/she left.

Variations

1.   Be very precise. Not only must Players be returned to their original seats but the Volunteer must also ask them to adopt the body positions and facial expressions they held as well.

2.   Set a time limit.

99.   REFLECTIONS

Starting from basic movements this can become an exercise in perfection with players working hard to mirror each other's movements exactly. As well as being a game in its own right it works well as a warm up exercise for mime.

Equipment

- None.

Setting up

1.   Put the group into pairs.
2.   The Players name themselves A and B.

Playing

1.   The A's and B's stand facing each other. A is to lead and B is to be the reflection.

2.   A performs (slowly at first) a sequence of movements and B must mirror these exactly as if he/she is the reflection of A in a mirror.

3.   Reverse roles and play again.

Variations

1.   Once the members of a group have had sufficient practice in this complex exercise in Pairs increase the numbers in each group so that a complex, multi-role mime is enacted and mirrored.

100. RELEASE

An extremely frenetic game that will wear out even the most energetic of players.

Equipment

*   None.

Setting up

1. Choose a number of Players to act as Catchers - a ratio of one to ten or fifteen depending on the group.

Playing

1. On your command the group spreads out and the Catchers try to catch as many Players as they can whilst Players try to avoid being caught.

2. Players are caught when a Catcher touches them.

3. Once a Player is caught he/she must go to the nearest wall and stand sideways an arms length away from it and stretch an arm out to touch it.

4. At any time during the game a Player can release a caught Player by passing between the caught Player and the wall under the caught Player's outstretched arm.

5. The game ends when everyone has been caught or when everyone collapses from exhaustion.

100.   RELEASE

Variations

1. If the game is being played outside the area of play must be clearly defined and captured Players simply stop when they have been caught and stand with their legs apart. Another Player must then pass between the legs of a captured Player to secure his/her release.

This can be difficult with very large groups - although not impossible - as the rhythm can be lost in the general noise. Persistence will allow such groups to develop sufficient skills to keep the rhythm and hear what is going on.

Equipment

- A chair for each Player.

Setting up

1. Sit everyone in a circle.
2. Choose a Starter.
3. Indicate the direction of play.

Playing

1. The Starter establishes a simple rhythm by using his/her body. The Starter can make vocal noises, clap hands, stamp feet or anything that is audible to the rest of the group.

2. The next Player adds to this rhythm with an additional noise of his/her own.

3. Each successive Player adds to this rhythm with his/her own additional noise.

4. This continues around the circle until each member of the whole group is contributing to a complex rhythm.

A degree of coordination is required to make this game successful. Thereafter, the poor old volunteer could well be in for a long stay in the centre of the circle.

Equipment

- A chair for each Player.
- A very long piece of string.
- A ring.

Setting up

1. Choose a Volunteer.
2. Sit everyone in a circle with the Volunteer in the middle.
3. Thread the ring onto the string before passing the string around the circle and then tie the ends so that the circle of string is the same size as the circle of Players.
4. Everyone in the circle takes hold of the string with both hands palm downwards as if they were holding the handlebars of a bicycle.

Playing

1. The Volunteer closes his/her eyes to allow movement of the ring to start.

2. The ring is moved around the circle of string hidden under the hands of the Players. It can go in either direction and Players may reverse the direction of travel whenever they wish.

   Undetected movement of the ring is best achieved if Players form the thumb and forefinger of each hand into a loose circle and curve their other fingers over to match. They should then adopt (in unison) a repeated gentle sliding movement which brings their hands together and then apart until they are touching their neighbours hands. This allows room for the ring to pass from Player to Player.

3. On your command the Volunteer opens his/her eyes and begins to look for the ring. If the Volunteer thinks he/she knows where it is at any given moment he/she must point to the Player that he/she thinks is concealing it.

4. When a Player is pointed to he/she must immediately take both hands from the string and hold them palms up to the Volunteer.

5. If the ring is not on the string the Volunteer remains in the middle and the game continues.

6. If the ring is revealed the Volunteer and Player swap places and the game begins again.

103. ROBOT

Human movement is extremely complex. It is all too easy to assume that a simple command is sufficient to elicit the required response. A suitably recalcitrant and literal 'robot', will soon prove that a great deal of thought will be needed to complete the simple task set by the game.

Equipment

- A chair for each player.
- A table.
- A cup of water.

Setting up

1. Sit the group in a semicircle.
2. Choose a Volunteer to be the Robot.
3. Sit the Robot between the horns of the semicircle facing the group.
4. Place the cup of water on the table some distance behind the Robot.

Playing

1. Each Player in succession is allowed to give the Robot one instruction.

2. The Robot must exactly follow any instruction given. The Robot is to be guided from its seat to the table where it is to pick up the cup and drink.

Variations

1. The nature of the instructions can be varied from the general - **stand up, turn left, walk, stop** to the precise - **raise left heel, keeping toes in contact with the ground, bending the left knee slightly** variety.

2. The nature of the task to be completed by the Robot can be altered.

The 'classic' trust exercise. But this game does a lot more than build trust, because when it is played properly, it is also extremely relaxing.

Equipment

*   None.

Setting up

1. Split the group into threes.
2. The Players name themelves A, B and C.

Playing

1   Players A and B stand facing one another with Player C between them facing either A or B.

2. Players A and B place their hands on the shoulders of Player C and rock C gently back and forth.

3. Player C must keep stiff rocking from heel to toe and not bending at the waist, knee or ankle.

4. Once Player C has gained confidence A and B can move a bit further apart so they have to let go of C as they rock him/her back and forth. It is important that Players A and B have their feet placed properly so that they are braced to take the weight of C as he/she falls against them.

5. Once C has gained sufficient confidence, he/she can close his/her eyes.

6. Swap roles so that all three Players have a chance to be rocked between the other two.

105. ROLL THE BODY

A development of *ROCK THE BODY,* this game takes the body rocking exercise a step further. Once the volunteers are sufficiently trustful of the other players they are in for a treat.

Equipment

- None.

Setting up

1. Put everyone into groups of ten or eleven.
2. Each group chooses a Volunteer.

Playing

1. The Volunteer stands on one spot and the other Players in that group form a tight circle around the Volunteer.

2. The Volunteer then falls in any direction of his/her choice keeping stiff as he/she falls and not bending at the waist, knee or ankle.

3. The Players in the circle catch the Volunteer and gently return him/her to an upright position whereupon the Volunteer falls in another direction.

4. This continues until the Volunteer has the confidence to close his/her eyes and fall gently in different directions and be passed back and forth across the circle with eyes shut.

5. Swap roles until each Player has had a chance to be in the middle.

6. When Players have become confident enough the circle can be widened so that the Volunteer has further to fall.

The success of this game depends largely on the subtlety of the answers given. It is best, therefore, when played with older players whose command of language and experience of life provides them with the wherewithal to answer both deviously and truthfully at the same time.

Equipment

* A chair for each Player.

Setting up

1. Sit everyone in a circle.
2. Choose a Volunteer.

Playing

1. The Volunteer leaves the room.

2. The members of the group decide on a rule. This can be anything they like but it must relate to the game.
    + *EXAMPLE: Answer as if you were the person on your right, always include . . . . . in your answer, do not use yes and no or always mention a film title. And so on.*

3. The Volunteer returns and asks each Player in turn one question. There is no limit to what the questions may be about.

4. Everyone must answer truthfully as well as obeying the rule.

5. The Volunteer must work out what the rule is before everyone has been questioned.

107.   SCULPTOR

A simple game that requires a fairly well developed understanding of human movement. It also requires a degree of control in order to keep to a given position - something artists' models will understand.

Equipment

- One chair for each pair of Players.

Setting up

1. Put everyone into pairs.
2. The Players name themselves A and B.

Playing

1. A is the Sculptor and in his/her own time moulds the B partner into any shape and position of his/her choice.

2. Reverse roles so that the B Player is the Sculptor who moulds A.

Variations

1. Increase the number in each of the groups so that the Sculptor has more material to work with.

2. Give Sculptors specific titles to work to.
   + *EXAMPLE: Royal wedding, flight, war, peace, heroes and heroines, and so on.*

There are many ways of coping with such a barrage of information as this game presents and making sense of it as well. Trying to pick out one item is not going to work, however, as that will not necessarily give any clue as to where it might be found.

Equipment

* A chair for each Player.

Setting up

1. Sit everyone in a circle.
2. Choose a Volunteer.

Playing

1. The Volunteer leaves the room.

2. The rest of the group decide upon a type of shop.
   + *EXAMPLE: Chemist, greengrocer, pet shop, hardware shop.*

3. Each Player then thinks of an item that can be bought in the shop selected by the group.
   + *EXAMPLE: If the shop is a Chemist such items as toothpaste, aspirin, film, soap and baby food might be chosen.*

4. The Volunteer returns to the room and stands in the centre of the circle.

5. At a signal from you everyone simultaneously shouts out the name of their chosen item as loudly as possible.

6. The Volunteer must try to identify the type of shop that was chosen by the group.

7.   If the Volunteer is unable to do so then the exercise is repeated except this time members of the group simultaneously whisper the names of their items.

8.   If a third attempt is necessary the names of the items are spoken at normal volume.

Variations

1.   Instead of types of shop specific locations such as a railway station, a park, a desert island, a zoo, a cinema, a school or a classroom can be chosen together with items that are found there.
     + *EXAMPLE: Railway station and classroom.*

LIST OF RAILWAY STATION ITEMS

Train

Platform

Track

Buffers

Sleepers

Tickets

Ticket office

Seat

Clock

Ticket collector

Porter

Passenger

Indicator board

Snack bar

Waiting room

Flower stall

Luggage

Litter bins

Busker

It is perhaps best to play this game with a smallish group as the language involved is unfamiliar. If players keep their same sign from game to game it is possible to work with larger numbers.

Equipment

- A chair for each Player.

Setting up

1. Sit everyone in a circle.
2. Choose a Starter.
3. Impose a strict rule of silence.

Playing

1. Each Player in turn invents a hand signal and shows it to the rest of the group.
   + *EXAMPLE: A chopping motion, finger waggling, slamming the fist of one hand into the palm of another, and so on.*

2. When everyone knows everyone else's sign the Starter begins by making his/her own sign and then another Player's sign.

3. The Player whose sign was made then makes his/her own sign and then someone else's sign.

4. The game continues in this way until someone makes a mistake, cannot think of another Player's sign or talks. This Player is then out and the game restarts with the previous Player.

5. This continues until only two Players remain.

Variations

1. Simplify the game by cutting out the intermediary stage of a Player making his/her own sign before making someone else's.

2. If all the members of the group keep the same sign from game to game try playing a more advanced version of the game by asking each Player to make the previous Player's sign first then his/her own sign next and someone else's after that.

110.   SORT OUT

Familiarity often confounds us. We look, but rarely see. How well, for example, could you describe what your partner or closest friend is wearing today?

Equipment

* A chair for each Player.

Setting up

1. Sit everyone in a circle.
2. Choose a Volunteer.
3. Send the Volunteer out of the room.

Playing

1. Once the Volunteer is out of the room ask the group to make a precise description of him/her and what he/she is wearing.

2. The Volunteer is called back into the room and the Players check the accuracy of their description.

Variations

1. You can ask the Volunteer (either as the Volunteer is leaving the room or at some earlier time) to make a subtle change to their appearance.

111. SOUNDAROUND

Many of the noises we can and do make are often the source of hilarity. This game is no exception and rarely makes it very far before someone laughs. It is, therefore, very good for bringing a group out of a tense or intense situation.

Equipment

* A chair for each Player.

Setting up

1. Sit everyone in a circle.
2. Choose a Starter.
3. Indicate the direction of play.

Playing

1. The Starter makes an abstract sound.

2. After a few seconds the next Player takes up the sound and then changes it without pausing - and when the Player does so the Starter becomes silent.

3. Each Player in turn takes up the the previous Player's noise and then changes it as the previous Player becomes silent. In this way you have a continuous but changing sound moving around the circle.

4. Anyone who laughs, talks or is struck dumb is out and the game begins again with the next Player.

112. SPEED TRIALS

This game gives you an opportunity to indulge your sadistic streak and whilst clapping very quickly soon weeds out most players, clapping very slowly can have the same effect.

Equipment

- None.

Setting up

1. Get everyone to stand in a place of their own as far from every other Player as possible.

Playing

1. Clap your hands - slowly at first.

2. Players must walk in time to your clapping one step per clap changing direction as necessary.

3. Vary the pace of your clapping gradually or suddenly as you see fit and change the Players pace.

4. The Players must try to avoid overbalancing or coming into contact with anyone else as they move about. Any Player who overbalances or touches another must stand still.

5. The game finishes when only one Player is still moving.

113.   SPELLBOUND

A group of players with extensive vocabularies will probably get more out of this game but it can provide a useful opportunity for those less confident to practise their skills.

Equipment

- A chair for each Player.

Setting up

1. Sit everyone in a circle.
2. Choose a Starter.
3. Indicate the direction of play.

Playing

1. The Starter says the name of any letter of the alphabet of his/her choice.
   + *EXAMPLE: Z.*

2. The next Player thinks of a word beginning with that letter and says the first letter chosen by the Starter and then adds the second letter of the word he/she is thinking of.
   + *EXAMPLE: If the Player is thinking of the word Zombie the Player says* **ZO.**

3. This continues around the circle with each person saying the previous compilation of letters and adding a letter to spell a word.

   The aim of the game is to extend the word as much as possible. Because of this it is most unlikely that the word that is finally spelt out will be the one that the first Player had in mind or members of the group were thinking of along the way.

+ *EXAMPLE: Z. ZO ZOO ZOOL ZOOLO ZOOLOG ZOOLOGI ZOOLOGIC ZOOLOGICA ZOOLOGICAL ZOOLOGICALL ZOOLOGICALLY.*

4. If a Player cannot extend a word any further that person is out but has the privilege of starting the next word with any letter of their choice.

Variations

1. For Players with good vocabularies allow letters to be added at the beginning of a word as well as at the end.
    + *EXAMPLE: Starter says A.*

    > *Player 1 says AL (ALARM)*
    > *Player 2 says TAL (TALISMAN)*
    > *Player 3 says STAL (STALLHOLDER)*
    > *Player 4 says ESTAL (PEDESTAL)*
    > *Player 5 says VESTAL.*
    > *The Sixth Player cannot extend the word and chooses the next starting letter.*

2. Add an element of bluff to the game by allowing Players to challenge one other by raising a hand if any Player is suspected of adding a letter that cannot eventually make a word. If the challenge is upheld the Player is out and if not the Challenger is out and the game starts again.

114. SPOT THE SPOT

This is one game that can drive groups to distraction, especially if the stickers are well camouflaged. It is also an indication of how well a group knows the way in which you think. If players are well tuned in to you, they will work out quite quickly where you are likely to have placed the stickers.

Equipment

- A sheet of small self-adhesive stickers of various shape, size and colour.

Setting up

1. Before the group enters the room stick a dozen or more of the spots in various places - well camouflaged but not unduly hidden.

Playing

1. Allow the group into the room.

2. Explain to the Players what you have done and tell them how many spots are hidden in the room.

3. Set the Players to finding the spots. The first person to find them all raises their hand and everyone stops while you check.

Variations

1. Whilst everyone is busy searching stick one of the spots on the back of one of the Players.

2. Be mean. Do not hide spots anywhere at all - do not mention the number of spots that have been hidden and see how long it is before any of the Players realise.

A straightforward game which is more or less a race between exhaustion and learning who is what.

Equipment

* A chair for each Player.
* A numbered list of towns - if there are twenty-four Players in the group use the first twenty-four towns on the list.

Setting up

1. Give each Player the name of a town. Whisper it so that no one else knows what it is.
2. Choose a Volunteer.
3. Sit everyone in a circle except the Volunteer who sits in the middle.
4. Give the list of towns to the Volunteer.

Playing

1. The Volunteer calls out the names of any two towns from the list - except for his/her own.

2. The two Players who bear the names of the towns called out must immediately get up and swap chairs.

3. The Volunteer must attempt to gain one of those seats.

4. Whoever is left standing must sit in the centre and call out two more names.

5. The game continues until everybody has worked out who is what and the game becomes too easy.

An exercise in concentration that works equally well as a warm up session for more complex work of a similar nature. Its scope is limited only by your ability to come up with similar sounding words to the commands.

Equipment

*   A chair for each Player.

Setting up

1.   Put the chairs into a large circle.
2.   Everyone stands inside the circle of chairs.

Playing

1.   When you say **Start** everyone starts to walk around within the circle.

2.   When you say **Stop** everyone must stop exactly where they are.

3.   Anyone who fails to obey these simple instructions is out and must leave the circle.

4.   Once this is established complicate matters by calling out false commands using such words as **Slop, Shop, Step, Stark, Star, Spark** or any other words that rhyme with or sound like **Stop** and **Start.**

5.   Anyone who reacts to a false command is out and must leave the circle.

6.   The game continues until all the Players are outside the circle.

Variations

1.   Introduce additional commands and words that sound similar to them.

Although based on an extremely simple and, probably, ancient premiss this game has endless potential to produce the most amazing, funny, serious, and surreal stories. It works well in its own right as a fun and powerful game but also has much to offer in terms of inspiration for other work.

Equipment

* A chair for each Player.

Setting up

1. Sit everyone in a circle.
2. Choose a Starter.
3. Indicate the direction of play.

Playing

1. The Starter makes up and tells the first sentence of a story.

2. The next Player makes up and tells a sentence to continue the story.

3. This carries on around the circle with each Player making a contribution to the growing story.

Variations

1. Instead of a sentence each Player can add a phrase or two sentences or more to whatever limit you wish to place.

2. Set a time limit for each Player instead of a word limit.

3. Try it all in gobbledegook.

118. TAKE-OFF AND LANDING

Perhaps the ultimate in trust games, this is where you go when groups have become blasé about the likes of *ROCK THE BODY* and *ROLL THE BODY*.

Equipment

- None.

Setting up

1. Choose a Volunteer.

Playing

1. The Volunteer retreats to the far end of the room.

2. The members of the group form two lines of equal number facing each other.

3. Each facing pair links hands by gripping their opposite number's wrists. This forms a long stretcher of arms.

4. When the Volunteer is ready he/she runs at the stretcher, dives into the air and lands full stretch on the linked arms of the members of the group.

5. Everyone takes a turn at taking off and landing.

As with *ROBOT* volunteers soon learn that what seem to be straightforward instructions can, when interpreted too literally, make matters far worse. Of course, much depends on the rest of the group but once players get used to the idea things can be very difficult indeed.

Equipment

- None.

Setting up

1. Choose a Volunteer.

2. Get the rest of the group to line up and hold hands forming a chain.

3. Indicate which Player is the head of the chain.

Playing

1. The Volunteer leaves the room.

2. The Player at the head of the chain leads the chain all around the room and then begins to tangle it by passing under arms, through legs and so on.

3. This continues until the chain is too tightly tangled to move.

4. The Volunteer returns to the room and must then attempt to untangle the chain using only spoken instructions. No touching is allowed.

The complicated execution of this game is worth persevering with as the results can often be extremely interesting. Once it has been played, groups know what to expect, hence the need - outlined in the variation - to increase the complexity of the game. Although this does not fool players for one minute, it greatly increases the chance for descriptions to mutate in the retelling.

Equipment

- A chair for each Player.

Setting up

1. Put everyone into pairs.
2. The Players name themselves A and B.
3. The A Players sit in a circle facing outwards.
4. The B Players sit in a circle facing inwards each opposite their partner.

Playing

1. All the A's look to their left and take note of the Player who is there (that is the A Player directly to their left) and then describe that person to their partner as accurately as they can.

2. All the B's move one place to their left and repeat the description they have just been given to their new partner. The description does not need to be repeated word for word but should be as accurate as possible.

3. All the B's move one more place to their left and the A's tell their new partners the description they have just been given. Again, not word for word but as accurately as possible.

4. Finally all the A's move two places to their right bringinq them back to their original partners who then recount the description they have just been given - which is meant to be a description of the person they are talking to.

Variations

2. Increase the number and complexity of moves involved ensuring only that the final position allows the description of a person to be given to that person.

121. TELLTALE TATTLE

This game has many names and is a perennial favourite that has a useful function. After all, with careful diction and a great deal of concentration, it is possible to 'defeat' the game. It is more fun, however, to see just how far from the original it is possible to stray.

Equipment

- A chair for each Player.

Setting up

1. Sit everyone in a circle.
2. Choose a Starter.
3. Indicate the direction of play.

Playing

1. Think of a word - preferably multi-syllabic and one with which the Players will be unfamiliar.

2. Whisper the word clearly in the ear of the Starter. You must whisper only once.

3. The Starter must then pass on the word that he/she thinks he/she heard in the same fashion to the next Player.

4. This happens right around the circle until the last person calls out the word as it arrived in their ear. It will very likely be different to the word you started with.

Variations

1. Instead of a word use a phrase or sentence.

2. Send a word, phrase or sentence in both directions at once.

3. A more complex variation of the game is to send round a short story.

4. In addition to sending round a short story this even more complex variation of the game has the entire group involved in some other activity while the short story is doing the rounds - this works as long as each player knows who to go to next.

Until players get the hang of this game, they will get hopelessly confused - which is part of the fun. It is an equivalent of the attempt to hop on one foot, pat your head with one hand and rub your stomach with the other. Once you can do it, it becomes easy and the trick then is to speed things up.

Equipment

- A chair for each Player.

Setting up

1. Sit everyone in a circle.
2. Choose a Starter.

Playing

1. The Starter points to a part of his/her own body and at the same time says it is some other part of their body and then adds the name of a Player in the circle.

   + *EXAMPLE: The Starter points to her elbow and says* **This is my knee, George.**

2. The named Player must point to whatever part of the body the previous Player called out and say it is some other part of the body and then add the name of another Player.

   + *EXAMPLE: Continuing with George. George points to his knee and says,* **This is my ear, Robin.** *Without hesitation Robin must then point to his ear and say,* **This is my . . . . .** *naming any part of the body except ear.*

3. This continues around the circle until a Player names what he/she points to, hesitates, gets confused or generally messes things up. This Player is then out and the game starts again with the previous Player.

We have all made wishes and know of the fairy tale convention of being granted three wishes. But there is also an old saying which says, 'Take care what you wish for, it might just come true'. This game is based on that idea and requires a great deal of imagination on the part of all the players. The volunteer must, after all, be very careful with the choice of wishes that are made, and the other players must come up with valid reasons that dramatically affect and change the way in which the wishes come true. There are many morals to be drawn from this game but most players will understand that without the need to have them pointed out.

Equipment

- A chair for each Player.

Setting up

1. Choose a Volunteer.
2. Sit everyone in a semicircle facing the Volunteer.
3. Choose a Starter who will speak first for the group.

Playing

1. Grant the Volunteer three wishes which must be made one at a time.
   + *EXAMPLE: 1st Wish Volunteer: I wish for a million pounds.*

2. When the first wish has been made the Players in the group must decide how the wish is to be granted.
   + *EXAMPLE: Starter: Your whole family is wiped out in a disaster and you are granted compensation of a million pounds in insurance money.*

3. If the Volunteer's first wish backfires then the second wish must be used to correct it.

   + *EXAMPLE: 2nd Wish Volunteer: I wish my family was still alive.*

4. Again the Players in the group must decide how the wish is to be granted.

   + *EXAMPLE: Player: You and your family are put in prison for trying to defraud the insurance company.*

5. The Volunteer must then use the third wish to get out of this situation.

   + *EXAMPLE: 3rd Wish Volunteer: I wish I hadn't been granted three wishes in the first place.*

6. Grant a new Volunteer three wishes and choose a different Starter to speak first for the group.

7. The game forces Players to use their wishes to extricate themelves from whatever situation they find themselves in and anyone who comes through three wishes unscathed is a winner.

Variations

1. This game can just as easily be played on a one to one basis.

124. THREE W'S

A variation on guessing games in which the questioner is limited to the types of question that can be asked. This makes the task much more difficult and increases the need for players to devise strategies to ask the sort of questions that will provide the greatest amount of information.

Equipment

* A chair for each Player.

Setting up

1. Sit everyone in a circle.
2. Choose a Volunteer.

Playing

1. The Volunteer leaves the room.

2. The other Players decide on the name of a person, place, or thing that the Volunteer must identify.

3. The Volunteer returns and must ask three questions of each Player to try and find out what was decided upon by the group.

4. The questions are limited in that the first must begin **When?** the second must begin **Why?** and the third must begin **Where?**

5. Whoever answers the question that finally allows the Volunteer to work out what it was must go out of the room and the game begins again.

Variations

1. Increase the number or change the words that questions begin with.

125. TOUCH STOP

More of a movement warm up than anything else, this can still be enormous fun and requires a great deal of skill.

Equipment

- Enough chairs to enclose a smallish area.

Setting up

1. Enclose an area large enough to hold about twice as many Players as there are in the group.
2. Put the group into the enclosure.

Playing

1. On your command everyone starts to move around.

2. If anyone touches anyone else both Players must stop moving.

3. The last Player moving is the winner.

Variations

1. Start with a larger enclosure and whilst the game is in progress make the enclosure smaller and smaller by moving chairs inwards.

Particularly effective with younger players this game can become extremely lively and noisy. With its silent ending, however, it is a very good way to finish a session and have all the players quiet and ready to leave.

Equipment

- A set of Animal Cards.
- A box to draw the cards from.

Setting up

1. Clear the room of all obstacles.
2. Place the cards in the box ensuring that there are two of each animal and that there are the same number of cards as Players.
3. Impose a strict rule of silence other than the single noise demanded of each Player by the game.
4. All the Players take a card to find out what animal they have become. They must not show the card to anyone else.
5. When everyone has chosen a card all the cards are returned to the box and the Players spread out.

Playing

1. Explain that you are Noah and that they are animals waiting to enter the Ark. However, they can only come in two-by-two.

2. On your command the Players must begin to move about the room looking for their partners.

3. As they are looking all the Players must imitate the noise of the animal they have become.

4. Once each Player has located their partner they line up in front of you in their twos completely still and silent.

126. TWO-BY-TWO

Equipment for variation 1

- Equipment to play sound effects.

Variations

1. Add to the atmosphere and the confusion by playing the sounds of rainfall and thunder.

2. Insist the pairs line up in alphabetical order according to the name of the animal.

LIST OF ANIMALS
Bee
Cat
Chicken
Cockerel
Cuckoo
Cow
Duck
Dog
Donkey
Elephant
Frog
Horse
Hyena
Lion
Monkey
Mouse
Owl
Pig
Sheep
Snake

127. US, THEM, BOYS, GIRLS

This game can tax the memory of the most dedicated of players as the group to which any particular player belongs can change and change back again a large of times.

Equipment

- A chair for each Player.

Setting up

1. Choose a Caller.
2. Sit everyone in a circle except the Caller who sits in the middle.

Playing

1. The Caller can call out one of four words: **Us**, **Them**, **Boys**, **Girls**.

2. The Players sitting in the circle must respond in the appropriate way to whichever word is called. The response alters depending on whether the Caller in the middle is a boy or girl.

CALL	RESPONSE TO BOY CALLER	RESPONSE TO GIRL CALLER
Us	Boys move	Girls move
Them	Girls move	Boys move
Boys	Boys move	Boys move
Girls	Girls move	Girls move

3. Players belonging to the group that has been called must all leave their chairs and find another one to sit on.

4. Whilst Players are swapping chairs the Caller must leave the seat in the middle and try to get one in the circle.

5. Whoever is left standing must take the central seat and call out one of the four words to start the next round.

6. Any Player who moves when he/she should not changes sex and must then obey calls accordingly.

+ *EXAMPLE: If the Caller is a girl and the call is **Us** and a boy moves. The boy who has moved at the wrong time becomes a girl and must move when the girls move.*

7. Any Player who fails to move when he/she should also changes sex and must then obey calls accordingly.

+ *EXAMPLE: If the Caller is a girl and the call is **Us** and a girl does not move. The girl who has failed to move becomes a boy and must then move when the boys move.*

8. The rest of the group must try to keep track of who is what because they must respond to the Caller in the correct manner.

+ *EXAMPLE: A boy who has become a girl who subsequently becomes the Caller and calls out **Us** must be responded to by girls only.*

Equipment for variation 1

• Coloured bands of the type used for sports for each Player.

Variations

1. To make the game simpler, if it is a same sex group or if members of the group cannot handle the idea of changing sex temporarily, split the group into two and mark the Players allegiance with coloured bands. Remember that Players who move at the wrong time must change their colours each time.

128.   VERBAL HIDE-AND-SEEK

Basically this is hide-and-seek for couch potatoes. Players need to think carefully about their surroundings and recall them with some precision. One of the advantages is that players do not actually have to be in a location that would in reality, be hidden from view.

Equipment

- A chair for each Player.

Setting up

1. Sit everyone in a circle.
2. Choose a Starter.

Playing

1. The Starter chooses a hiding place that is known to the rest of the Players in the group.

2. Each Player in turn asks a question of the Starter in an attempt to discover where the Starter is hiding.

3. The Starter may only answer **Yes** or **No**.

4. Whichever Player finds the Starter by correctly stating where he/she believes the Starter to be hiding then takes a turn at hiding and the game starts again.

Variations

1. In addition to choosing the hiding place the Starter can hide an object there. Once the Players have established the hiding place they must then identify the object hidden there in the same manner.

As with other such games as *RING ON A STRING*, players are more likely to reveal that they have the coin in their possession through the expression on their face.

Equipment

- A chair for each Player.
- A long refectory style table.
- A coin or similar token.

Setting up

1. Divide the group into two Teams and sit the Players facing each other across the table.
2. Give the coin to one of the Teams.

Playing

1. On your command Players in the Team with the coin pass it back and forth along the line under the table.

2. After a set time (ten or fifteen seconds is the usual) any Player on the opposing Team can call out **Which fist?** when the Player thinks he/she knows who has the coin.

3. At that all the Players on the Team with the coin must place their hands in fists on the table.

4. The Player who called out **Which fist?** must now point to the fist of the Player who he/she thinks is concealing the coin and must say **That fist!**

5. The Player pointed at must then open the fist to reveal whether or not the coin is concealed there. If the Player has the coin it goes to the other Team and the game starts again with the Team that started with the coin in opposition. If the Player does not have the coin the Player who called out **Which fist? That fist!** is out and the original Team replace their fists under the table and continue to pass the coin until they are challenged again.

Variations

1. If a table is not available the game can be played sitting on the floor. If the Teams are sitting on the floor the Players will have to pass the coin behind their backs. Also, Players on the Team with the coin must place their hands in fists on the floor in front of them when a challenge is made.

130. WHO, ME?

It is extremely difficult to break the everyday conventions of personal communication as this game will display. The temptation to answer a question directed at you is overwhelming and the problem is compounded by the fact that you have to trust the person who is answering for you.

Equipment

- A chair for each Player.

Setting up

1. Choose a Volunteer.
2. Sit everyone in a circle except the Volunteer who sits in the middle.

Playing

1. The Volunteer says to the rest of the Players **From now on you must not answer any question I ask you. The person on your left must answer for you.** The Volunteer then points to someone and says **Do you understand?**

2. If the Player answers the question he/she is out.

3. The game continues in this way with the Volunteer pointing to Players and asking questions. Each time the Player on their left must answer for them. Anyone answering a question directed at them is out.

Variations

1. Forbid the use of the words **Yes** and **No** in any answer.

131. WHO'S NEXT?

Experienced players can play this game at lightning speed but it only takes a momentary lapse of concentration for someone to be panicked into the wrong move. It is sometimes easier to play a game like this by not concentrating too hard. Too much thought can slow your responses.

Equipment

- A chair for each Player.

Setting up

1. Sit everyone in a circle.
2. Choose a Starter.

Playing

1. The Starter points to any other Player in the circle and says **Who's next?**

2. The Player pointed at must respond in one of two ways depending on how the Starter pointed.

3. If the Starter points with the left hand the Player pointed at must immediately name the player sitting to their left and ask **Who's next?**

4. If the Starter points with the right hand the Player pointed at must immediately name the player sitting to their right and ask **Who's next?**

5. The Player named must then point to another Player using either hand and then name that person and ask **Who's next?**

6. A Player may point to anyone except the Player who has just named him/her.

7. Any Player who hesitates, points to the wrong Player, or gets a name wrong is out. Then the Player who should have been next starts the next game.

132. WHO? WHAT?

An exercise in using language creatively to give as much information as possible whilst making it as difficult as possible to use that information to identify the object in question. We are all quite good at this but it is interesting to see how far it can be taken.

Equipment

- A chair for each Player.

Setting up

1. Put everyone into pairs.
2. The Players name themselves A and B.

Playing

1. A Players choose a person or object in the room without revealing it.

2. The A's give B's a clue about the identity of the chosen person or object.

3. When a clue is given B must attempt to name the person or object.

4. B is allowed up to ten clues which can be as obscure as A can manage to make them.

5. When B has guessed correctly or has run out of clues reverse roles and play again.

Variations

1. The number of clues can be varied but too many make for a dull game.

2. Do not restrict the game to people or objects in the room.

133. WORD ASSOCIATION

An ancient game that can be played in many situations between partners or in groups. The joy is in coming up with associations that may be obscure but are, nonetheless, legitimate.

Equipment

- A chair for each Player.

Setting up

1. Sit everyone in a circle.
2. Choose a Starter.
3. Indicate the direction of play.

Playing

1. The Starter calls out the name of any object whatsoever.

2. The next Player must immediately call out a word that is connected in some way with the previous one.

3. This continues round and round the circle.

4. If a Player hesitates or repeats the name of an object already mentioned that Player is out.

5. If a Player makes a dubious connection any other Player can challenge this. The Player who has been challenged must then justify the choice of word by connecting it in some way with the previous one. If the challenged Player can do so he/she stays in the game and it continues. If the challenged Player cannot he/she is out and the game starts again with the next Player.

+ *EXAMPLE: Starter:* **Frog**

Player 1: **March**

Player 2: **Hare**

Player 3: **Cut**

Player 4: **Playing cards**

Player 5: **Joker**

Player 6: **Batman**

Player 7: **Robin**

Player 8: **Woodpecker**

Player 9: **Woodlouse**

Player 10: **Fourteen**

Player 11 Challenges Player 10.

Player 10 Explains that a woodlouse has 14 legs and stays in the game.

Player 11: Is out of the game.

Player 12: **One**

Player 13: **Race**

Player 14: **Runner**

Player 15: **Bean**

Player 16: **Not a bean**

Player 1: **Zilch**

Player 2: **Nothing**

Player 3: **Black hole**

Player 4: **Pink hole**

Player 3: Challenges Player 4.

Player 4: Insists that a hole can be any colour. It is put to the vote and Player 4 is out.

Player 5: Starts the game again.

Variations

1. Try playing *WORD DISASSOCIATION* in which the rules are the same except that each word must have no connection whatsoever with the previous one.

134. WINKING

This game requires an odd number of players to be divided into two groups, one group having one more player than the other. If the group should divide into boys and girls like this, all to the good, but this is not essential.

Equipment

- The same number of chairs as Players in the larger group.

Setting up

1. Put the chairs into a circle.
2. Get the smaller group to sit down. This will leave one chair empty.
3. Players in the larger group stand outside the circle facing inward one Player behind each chair. The Starter is the person standing behind the empty chair.

Playing

1. The Starter begins the game by winking at any Sitting Player of his/her choice.

2. The Sitting Player who is winked at must immediately leave their chair and run to the empty one.

3. As the Sitting Player stands the Player standing behind that chair must try to stop him/her leaving. This is done by touching their shoulder.

4. If the standing Player succeeds the Sitting Player must sit down in the original seat and the Starter must try again.

5. If the Player standing behind the Sitting Player who is winked at fails to stop the Sitting Player from getting away he/she will be left standing behind an empty seat. It is now the standing Player's turn to wink at someone and try to get the seat in front occupied.

135. YES AND NO

There are some words so common to our everyday usage that we can easily twist ourselves into knots when we try to avoid using them.

Equipment

* A large number of dried peas or similar objects.

Setting up

1. Give each Player five peas.

Playing

1. On your command everyone mills around engaging each other in conversation.

2. If one Player succeeds in making another Player use the words **Yes** or **No** then the successful Player must give the other a pea as a forfeit.

3. Once a **Yes** or **No** has been uttered and the pea given as forfeit the two Players break up and find new Players to engage in conversation.

4. The first Player to lose all their peas is the winner.

Variations

1. Change the words to be avoided.
   + *EXAMPLE: Me and You, Left and Right, or Up and Down.*

2. Play it one to one instead of in a group.

3. Increase the number of peas to be got rid of.

And finally, after playing any or all of these games .... time to take a well deserved zizz.

ZIZZ/ZIZ/ *n. & v.colloq. English.* •*n.* 1. **a short sleep**.

•*v.* 2. **doze or sleep.** [imitative.] catnap, doze or sleep lightly for a short time, drop off, drowze, take forty winks, kip, nap, nod off, snooze, shuteye, ...

ADDITIONAL TITLES

All books may be ordered direct from:

DRAMATIC LINES   PO BOX 201   TWICKENHAM   TW2 5RQ ENGLAND
UK freephone orderline: 0800 5429570
tel: +44(0)20 8296 9502
fax: +44(0)20 8296 9503
e-mail: mail@dramaticlinespublishers.co.uk
www.dramaticlines.co.uk

MONOLOGUES

THE SIEVE AND OTHER SCENES
Heather Stephens
ISBN 0 9522224 0 X

The Sieve contains unusual short original monologues valid for junior acting examinations. The material in The Sieve has proved popular with winning entries worldwide in drama festival competitions. Although these monologues were originally written for the 8-14 year age range they have also been used by adult actors for audition and performance pieces. Each monologue is seen through the eyes of a young person with varied subject matter including tough social issues such as fear, 'Television Spinechiller', senile dementia, 'Seen Through a Glass Darkly' and withdrawal from the world in 'The Sieve'. Other pieces include: 'A Game of Chicken', 'The Present', 'Balloon Race' and a widely used new adaptation of Hans Christian Andersen's 'The Little Match Girl' in monologue form.

CABBAGE AND OTHER SCENES
Heather Stephens
ISBN 0 9522224 5 0

Following the success of The Sieve, Heather Stephens has written an additional book of monologues with thought provoking and layered subject matter valid for junior acting examinations. The Cabbage monologues were originally written for the 8-14 year age range but have been used by adult actors for audition and performance pieces. The Aberfan slag-heap disaster issues are graphically confronted in 'Aberfan Prophecy' and 'The Surviving Twin' whilst humorous perceptions of life are observed by young people in 'The Tap Dancer' and 'Cabbage'. Other pieces include: 'The Dinner Party Guest', 'Nine Lives' and a new adaptation of Robert Browning's 'The Pied Piper' seen through the eyes of the crippled child.

MONOLOGUES

ALONE IN MY ROOM ORIGINAL MONOLOGUES   Ken Pickering

ISBN 0 9537770 0 6

This collection of short original monologues includes extracts from the author's longer works in addition to the classics. Provocative issues such as poverty and land abuse are explored in 'One Child at a Time', 'The Young Person Talks' and 'Turtle Island' with adaptations from 'Jane Eyre', Gulliver's Travels' and 'Oliver Twist' and well-loved authors including Dostoyevsky. These monologues have a wide variety of applications including syllabus recommendation for various acting examinations. Each monologue has a brief background description and acting notes.

FEMININE ZONES ORIGINAL SOLO SCENES   Sharon McCoy

ISBN 0 9537770 9 X

A collection of 40 original and contemporary monologues of our time, highlighting relationship issues for teenagers and young women. Sharon McCoy writes in a fresh, thoughtful and powerful way about situations we can all relate to and will be evocative for all those who read, watch or perform. The monologues range between 1 – 3 minutes in length making them ideal for showcases pieces and audition call backs in both the UK and USA. The material is equally suitable for many speech and drama examinations and recommended for the Trinity Guildhall syllabus as well as having a wide variety of theatrical and school curriculum uses including personal and social development studies.

DUOLOGUES

PEARS   Heather Stephens

ISBN 0 9522224 6 9

Heather Stephens has written layered, thought provoking and unusual short original duologues for speech and drama festival candidates in the 8-14 year age range. The scenes have also been widely used for junior acting examinations and in a variety of school situations and theatrical applications. Challenging topics in Pears include the emotive issues of child migration, 'Blondie', 'The Outback Institution' and bullying 'Bullies', other scenes examine friendship, 'The Best of Friends', 'The Row' and envy, 'Never the Bridesmaid'. New duologue adaptations of part scenes from the classic play, 'Peace' by Aristophanes and classic novel 'Oliver Twist' by Charles Dickens are also included.

TOGETHER NOW ORIGINAL DUOLOGUES   Ken Pickering

ISBN 0 9537770 1 4

This collection of short duologues includes extracts from Ken Pickering's longer works together with new original pieces. The variety of experiences explored in the scenes are those which we can all easily identify with such as an awkward situation, 'You Tell Her', and the journey of self knowledge in 'Gilgamesh' whilst pieces such as 'Mobile phones', 'Sales' and 'Food' observe realistic situations in an interesting and perceptive way. Other duologues are based on well-known stories including 'Snow White' and John Bunyan's classic work 'The Pilgrim's Progress'. Each piece has a brief background description and acting notes and the scenes have syllabus recommendation for a number of examination boards as well as a wide variety of theatrical and school applications.

SHAKESPEARE THE REWRITES
Claire Jones
ISBN 0 9522224 8 5

A collection of short monologues and duologues for female players taken from rewrites of Shakespeare plays from 1670 to the present day, written by authors embellishing original texts for performances, adding prequels or sequels or satisfying very personal ideas about production. These fresh and unusual scenes provide exciting auditions and examinations material. Comparisons with the original Shakespeare text are fascinating and this book will provide a useful contribution to Theatre Study work from GCSE to beyond 'A' level. Contributors include: James Thurber (Macbeth) Arnold Wesker (Merchant of Venice) and Peter Ustinov (Romanoff and Juliet), and a most unusual Japanese version of Hamlet.

SCENES FOR TWO TO TEN PLAYERS

JELLY BEANS
Joseph McNair Stover
ISBN 0 9522224 7 7

The distinctive style and deceptively simple logic of American writer Joseph McNair Stover has universal appeal with scenes that focus on young peoples relationships in the contemporary world and vary in tone from whimsical to serious. The collection of 9 original 10-15 minute scenes for 2, 3 and 4 players is suitable for 11 year olds through to adult. Minimal use of sets and props makes them easy to stage and also ideal for group acting examinations, classroom drama, assemblies and various other theatrical applications. These pieces have also been used with success at Young Writers Workshops to teach the elements of script writing and dramatic development.

SCENES FOR TWO TO TEN PLAYERS

HARD BOILED
Joseph McNair Stover
ISBN 1 904557 17 1

After the success of Jelly beans American writer Joseph McNair Stover has written more scenes focussing on young peoples relationships in his distinctive style – introducing characters such as a 1930's private investigator, strangers in a park, sisters and characters without names. The collection of 5 original 10-20 minute scenes for 1 character plus a male voice, 2, 3, 5 and 7 players is suitable for 11 year olds through to adult. As with Jelly Beans minimal use of sets and props makes them ideal for group acting examinations, classroom drama, assemblies and various other theatrical applications.

SCENES 4 3 2 10 PLAYERS
Sandy Hill
ISBN 0 9537770 8 1

Sandy Hill has written this collection of 10 original scenes for 3 to 10 players with opportunities for doubling-up of characters and introduction of optional additional players. Scenes are often quirky and vary in tone with unusual endings. The versatile scenes are of various playing times and suitable for performers from as young as 7 through to adult. The flexible use of sets and props have made these pieces particularly useful for group acting examinations and have proved to be immediately popular and successful for candidates as well as winning entries at drama festivals, and they can also be used effectively for classroom drama and school assemblies.

WILL SHAKESPEARE SAVE US! 　　　　　Paul Nimmo
WILL SHAKESPEARE SAVE THE KING! 　　ISBN 0 9522224 1 8

Famous speeches and scenes from Shakespeare are acted out as part of a comic story about a bored king and his troupe of players in 2 versatile plays. Both plays are suitable for the 11-18 year age range and have been produced with varying ages within the same cast and also performed by adults to a young audience. The plays can be produced as a double bill, alternatively each will stand on its own, performed by a minimum cast of 10 without a set, few props and modern dress or large cast, traditional set and costumes. The scripts are ideal for reading aloud by classes or groups and provide an excellent introduction to the works of Shakespeare. Both plays have been successfully performed on tour and at the Shakespeare's Globe in London.

SUGAR ON SUNDAYS AND OTHER PLAYS 　　Andrew Gordon
ISBN 0 9522224 3 4

A collection of 6 one act plays bringing history alive through drama. Events are viewed through the eyes of ordinary people and each play is packed with details about everyday life, important events and developments of the period. All 40-50 minute plays can be used as classroom drama, for school performances, shared texts for the literacy hour and group acting examinations. The plays are suitable for Key Stage 2 upwards. and explore Ancient Egypt, Ancient Greece, Anglo-Saxon and Viking Times, Victorian Britain and the Second World War. A glossary of key words helps to develop children's historical understanding of National Curriculum History Topics and the plays provide opportunities for children to enjoy role-play and performance.

X-STACY 　　　　　　　　　　　　　Margery Forde
ISBN 0 9522224 9 3

Margery Forde's powerful play centres on the rave culture and illicit teenage drug use and asks tough questions about family, friends and mutual responsibilities. The play has proved hugely successful in Australia where it was originally produced with a cast of 7. It is suitable for both amateur and professional performance and versatile, with opportunity to include a non-speaking crowd and write in additional characters. This English edition is published with extensive teachers' notes to enrich its value for the secondary school classroom, PSHE studies, English and drama departments in schools and colleges.

WHAT IS THE MATTER WITH MARY JANE? 　　Wendy Harmer
ISBN 0 9522224 4 2

This monodrama about a recovering anorexic and bulimic takes the audience into the painful reality of a young woman afflicted by eating disorders. The play is based on the personal experience of actress Sancia Robinson and has proved hugely popular in Australia. It is written with warmth and extraordinary honesty and the language, humour and style appeal to current youth culture. A study guide for teachers and students is included in this English edition ensuring that the material is ideal for use in the secondary school classroom and for PSHE studies, drama departments in schools and colleges in addition to amateur and professional performance.

THREE CHEERS FOR MRS BUTLER

adapted by Vicky Ireland
ISBN 0 9537770 4 9

This versatile musical play about everyday school life is for anyone who has ever been to school. It features the poems and characters created by Allan Ahlberg with a foreword by Michael Rosen, songs by Colin Matthews and Steven Markwick and was first performed at the Polka Theatre for Children, London. The 2 acts of 40 minutes each can be performed by children, adults or a mixture of both, and the play can be produced with a minimum cast of 7 or a large cast of any size, with or without music and all 19 songs, as well as having a wide variety of other musical and dramatic applications.

THREE CHEERS FOR MRS BUTLER CD

backing tracks 19 songs

FRIENDLY MATCHES
a play of two halves!

dramatised by Vicky Ireland
ISBN 1 904557 16 3

This cleverly conceived versatile musical play is clever and funny and is for anyone who has ever played or watched school football. It features poems and characters created by Allan Ahlberg and the story follows the fortunes of a failing football team and its coach, school staff and parents and introduces football teams comprised of highly unlikely historical characters. The two acts of 40 minutes each can be performed by children of Primary age and older, adults or a mixture of both and produced with a minimum cast of 7 or a large cast of any size, with or without music and songs.

FRIENDLY MATCHES CD

backing tracks 19 songs and instrumentals

INTRODUCING OSCAR
The Selfish Giant & The Happy Prince

Veronica Bennetts
ISBN 0 9537770 3 0

Oscar Wilde's timeless stories for children have been chosen for adaptation because of the rich opportunities offered for imaginative exploration and the capacity to vividly illuminate many aspects of the human condition. The original dialogue, lyrics and music by Veronica Bennetts can be adapted and modified according to the needs of the pupils, individual schools or groups. The Selfish Giant runs for 25 minutes and The Happy Prince for 1 hour 15 minutes. Both musicals can be used for Trinity Guildhall examinations and make ideal end of term productions for drama groups and primary and secondary schools.

INTRODUCING OSCAR 2 CD pack

The Selfish Giant: backing tracks 11 songs and instrumentals
The Happy Prince: backing tracks 19 songs and instrumentals

ADVENT JOURNEY

Ken Pickering
ISBN 1 904557 18X

This unusual Christmas musical show featuring an Advent Calendar with characters and objects appearing from the windows takes the form of a journey towards the light at Bethlehem in an otherwise dark world. The play can be staged in almost any space without a set and simple props, or a formal set with lavish costumes. Casting is flexible with almost all 29 played by either sex. The option to add or double-up, with opportunity to redistribute lines, and use additional musicians and dancers, makes it an ideal Primary School or Church Christmas production, performed by a class, mixed age cast or by adults for an audience of children.

ADVENT JOURNEY 2 CD pack   backing tracks 11 songs and instrumentals
vocal backing tracks 19 songs and instrumentals

DRAMA LESSONS IN ACTION

Antoinette Line
ISBN 0 9522224 2 6

Resource material suitable for classroom and assembly use for teachers of junior and secondary age pupils. Lessons are taught through improvisation. These are not presented as 'model lessons' but provide ideas for adaptation and further development. The lessons include warm-up and speech exercises and many themes are developed through feelings such as timidity, resentfulness, sensitivity and suspicion. The material can be used by groups of varying sizes and pupils are asked to respond to interesting texts from a diverse selection of well known authors including: Roald Dahl, Ogden Nash, Ted Hughes, Michael Rosen, Oscar Wilde and John Betjeman.

DRAMA•DANCE•SINGING
TEACHER RESOURCE BOOK

edited by John Nicholas
ISBN 0 9537770 2 2

Phillip Schofield has written the foreword for this collection of drama, dance and singing lesson activities that have been drawn from a bank of ideas used by the Stagecoach Theatre Arts Schools teachers. Lessons include speech and drama exercises, games and improvisations often developed as a response to emotions. Dance activities include warm-ups, basic dance positions, improvisations, versatile dance exercises and routines while singing activities help to develop rhythm and notation as well as providing enjoyable games to develop the voice. Activities can be adapted for large or small group use and are suitable for 6 - 16 year olds in a fun yet challenging way.

ONE CHILD AT A TIME

Ken Pickering

THE IMMORTAL HARVEY

Ken Pickering

Three scenes from the Alone in my Room monologues are taken from One Child at a Time and The Immortal Harvey.

ASSEMBLIES! ASSEMBLIES! ASSEMBLIES!

Kryssy Hurley
ISBN 0 9537770 6 5

These teacher-led assemblies require minimum preparation and have been written by a practising teacher to involve small or large groups. Each assembly lasts 15 - 20 minutes and is suitable for Key Stages 2 and 3. Many PSHE and Citizenship issues are explored, including bullying, racism, friendship, co-operation, feeling positive, making responsible choices and decisions, school rules and laws outside school. There are 12 assemblies for each term and all have the following sections: Resources and Organisation, What to Do, Reflection Time and Additional Resources and Activities.

DRAMATIC LINES HANDBOOKS

in association with Trinity Guildhall The International Examinations Board

The handbooks are primarily designed to support students and teachers by providing accessible and practical advice for anyone working towards ANY examination in Drama, Speech, Communication or the Performing Arts.

ACTING SHAKESPEARE FOR AUDITIONS AND EXAMINATIONS

Frank Barrie
ISBN 1 904557 10 4

This invaluable and readable handbook by actor, director and Senior Assessor in Speech and Drama, Frank Barrie examines eleven selected audition speeches from Shakespeare's plays: the background to each speech, examination of the character, the meaning of the lines and suggestions as to their delivery, together with explanation of the meaning of archaic words plus points of interest and advice. Practical aspects including exercises, choosing speeches, how to behave and what to wear at auditions, and common faults are also covered.

SPEECH AND DRAMA

Ann Jones & Robert Cheeseman
ISBN 1 904557 15 5

All the elements to teaching approaches in speech and drama are carefully explored in this highly acclaimed handbook written by two distinguished and successful practitioners which is designed to provide practical advice to teachers and students preparing for Speech and Drama examinations. This book will benefit anyone with an interest in Speech and Drama, poetry and prose speaking, improvisation, prepared and sight reading, choral speaking, prepared and impromptu talks are included and enriching practical work is suggested by understanding facts and principals including phrasing, relaxation and resonance.

THINKING ABOUT PLAYS

Ken Pickering & Giles Auckland-Lewis
ISBN 1 904557 14 7

Speech and Drama, Acting or Theatre examination candidates will almost certainly be asked questions that provide an opportunity to show what they think about plays. This handbook is a particularly useful guide for Drama and Speech students as it does not tell the reader WHAT to think but HOW to think about plays. Carefully chosen sections in this handbook ask the reader to consider aspects such as text, form, structure and stage design in both classical and modern theatre. This book will help teachers and students to think about a wide variety of plays whether writing about them, performing or directing productions.

PREPARING FOR YOUR DIPLOMA
IN DRAMA AND SPEECH

Kirsty N Findlay & Ken Pickering
ISBN 1 904557 00 7

John Gardyne, the Trinity Guildhall Chief Examiner in Drama and Speech Subjects has edited this invaluable new edition and he provides invaluable updates, additional information and guidance for anyone following a current Drama and Speech course. Preparing For Your Diploma is full of sound advice about preparing for performer's and teaching diplomas. The easy to follow topics include taking practical examinations, answering written papers, shaping, writing and editing work, academic referencing and structuring a bibliography. Kirsty N Findlay and Ken Pickering have a wealth of experience in providing support for students and teachers and have written in an informal style that establishes an immediate dialogue with the reader.

MUSICAL THEATRE

Gerry Tebbutt
ISBN 1 904557 12 0

This handbook is essential for all those with a serious interest in Musical Theatre. The book aims to equip students with the necessary information to pursue a career in Musical Theatre and covers first experiences, through Drama School to becoming a fully-fledged professional. Gerry Tebbutt asks pertinent questions of the reader in order to examine the motives for choosing to be in Musical Theatre and he explores the various forms, from the birth of musical comedy to current trends, in order to stress the importance of understanding the industry. Practical suggestions include advice on getting into Drama School, and choices and suitability of different types of songs and speeches for auditions.

EFFECTIVE COMMUNICATION

John Caputo, Jo Palosaari & Ken Pickering
ISBN 1 904557 13 9

'Communication' embraces a wide range of situations including the skills of public speaking, debating, discussing, listening, counselling, mediating, negotiating and marketing. This comprehensive handbook is for anyone who cares about good oral communication through the medium of the English language. It will be particularly useful to those who are undertaking assessment or an examination in communication or public speaking. Each section suggests how it can be used best as some readers may wish to focus only on particular communication aspects like interpersonal skills or language and sound. Methods of effective communication are explored in a wide range of contexts and the reader is invited to participate in a programme of self-development. The book is also extremely useful for those who are acquiring English as an additional language.